## •• CANOEIN

2

# THE BEAUTIFUL SUWANNEE RIVER!

A TRUE STORY . . . of

Canoeing and camping on the Suwannee River from Fargo, GA., to the Gulf of Mexico . . . Pristine beauty beyond description . . . Abundant Wildlife . . . 'gators and 100 lb. acrobatic fish.

– Including –

A brief history of famed story teller Lem Griffis and his Griffis Fish Camp on the edge of the swamp, where this story got its beginning, **40 years ago!**

— THIS EDITION ALSO INCLUDES —

A short
**History of the great Okefenokee Swamp,**
headwaters of the Suwannee River, and its inhabitants.

Tips on buying a canoe, tips on canoe and river safety, a canoe camper's check list, and name, address and phone numbers of river outfitters.

A Professionally edited **VHS VIDEO** is also available covering the whole river _and_ the two Okefenokee swamp trips. It lets you see the beauty of the swamp, the river and campsites for yourself. It covers most of the places discussed in this book.

**Ask your dealer for it.**
If he cannot supply it,
you may order by calling 407-636-4949
or Faxing 407-635-8615

ii

Published by

William A. Logan
1512 Cambridge Dr.
Cocoa, Florida 32922
Ph. 407-636-4949
FAX 407-635-8615

# Second Edition

0-9665500-0-5
ISBN NUMBER

# Preface

The intent of this **Canoeing and Camping** story is to give those who are planning on canoeing the Suwannee River as much useful camping and canoeing information as possible from **our** trip. Regarding general distances, paddling times, points of interest, where there are, *or are not* good primitive campsites, re-supply points, and a little insight—what to expect, etc. Hopefully, so that the readers may be better informed and can enjoy their river trip with the least amount of problems.

Though this book was written *mainly* for the information and enjoyment of those who are considering experiencing the Suwannee River *for the first time*, I'm sure those more experienced Suwannee River travelers will also find something useful as well.

Canoes offer an excellent family-outing for families with older children. There is ample opportunity to play, converse, and work together to achieve a goal. This outdoor recreation which goes from creeks to riverbanks to rapids can be quite tame or very exciting.

Canoes are quiet. Wild animals wait longer to flee from a canoe giving you a chance to see these animals or, occasionally, even observe them closely. Canoes also give you an opportunity to commune with nature, even camp along the riverbank for a night or a week. Almost any area of the U.S. can offer a nearby canoeing opportunity.

While it can be boring to canoe a low-water river, it can also be dangerous to canoe a flooded river. Experienced canoers can navigate a river that is swollen with rains and running rapidly. It is a good idea for the rest of us to wait for the water to subside somewhat.

Near the back of this book, you will find people, places and products recommended. In several cases, references to them in a manner that you could interpret as advertising a company or its products; i.e., I mention a particular repellent several places. **In no way** have I made any "deals" with those mentioned. References to them, their product or service, is <u>my own</u> recommendation, without compensation <u>*of any kind.*</u>

My intent is only to inform what I found to be a good product or service. (Such as the good restaurant we found.) Also, on this subject, in this book I describe the services of *only one* specific CANOE OUTFITTER on the River. Mainly, because of their location to the upper reaches of the river and the fact that they gave us great service. Picking us up 85 miles away at our Gulf pullout point and arriving within five minutes of *our arrival.* That's great service!

Furthermore, I do not wish to imply there are not other equally as good or as qualified Outfitters and Canoe Rental Companies on the river. There are *many* and I'm sure their services are also quite good. Check your phone directory. However, since I did not use their services, I didn't feel I could describe them fairly in the first edition. I explain the above since I had one fellow chastise me severely for what he called "advertising" and not mentioning *other* Canoe Outfitters on the river. He was rather upset since his business was not mentioned.

Trying to please everyone (though we know that is not possible) I list those major outfitters I have information on, near the back of this edition.

## DEDICATION

I dedicate this book to my loving wife, Joyce, without whose love, understanding and tolerance, this book might never have been written. And to my new found friends, **Harry McDonald, Randy Pieper, Ray DeFillips, O. Van Orman, and Ron Bussendorf,** who decided to accompany me on my trip down river. They were all good sports, loads of laughs and made excellent canoeing companions.

## CREDITS

I wish to also thank **Bill Sargent** of the **Florida Today News** in Brevard County for writing the "Outdoor" stories that resulted in those fine fellows joining me on my adventure down this beautiful river. Without his help, I also might never have written this book.

Thank you Bill

Credit also goes to **Marla Weech,** of Orlando's **WFTV-Channel 9 News,** for airing her **"Florida – by Paddle, Pack and Pedal,"** where she showed a segment of canoeing Florida's Rivers. It was *this* show that rekindled my desire and determination to do what I had wanted to do . . . 40 years ago!

Thank you Marla!

Special thanks to **Professor Chris T. Trowell** of South Georgia College, Douglas, Georgia, (Professor Trowell is a well known and respected "Historian of the Okefenokee") for contributing the history of the swamp and its inhabitants. His help has been invaluable. I found the other sources of information I had used in my "Thumbnail History" for my First Edition were not reliable.

Thank you Chris!

I would like to also thank Terry Jensen of Cybersports (on the Internet) for allowing me to reprint their copyrighted article on "Buying a Canoe" on page 85.

I also wish to thank management of the **Suwannee River Water Management District** for allowing me to reproduce their great maps of the Suwannee River and **GPS** information on the springs.

## AUTHOR'S NOTE!

After the trip, we found the map we had used, to be the **_first_** map issued by the Suwannee River Water Management District. It was a large pale blue on white, titled SUWANNEE RIVER **_"CANOE MAP"_** . . . It was mistitled! It only covered launch ramp locations relative to roads, highways, etc. We found it had _very little_ useful information to the person **on** _the river._ However, it did give distances to major locations and _that_ was useful. There is now a _newer version_ called SRWMD "Boat Ramps & Canoe Launch" map. They are also waterproof and have **far** more information than the one _we_ used. However, for canoers and boaters, I would like to see more **river landmarks and springs** that are located **on** the river incorporated into those maps. I have included a map of the approximate location on the springs to give you some idea where to look for them. For those who are fortunate enough to own a new GPS . . . I have included the GPS location coordinates supplied to me by SRWMD. These should pinpoint the location for you. Hopefully, SRWMD will include these (the springs) in future printings.

Though **The Suwannee River Management District** allowed me to reprint their map, due to the size of the pages and limited space, I was not able to include the **key text** describing how to reach the boat ramps by car. If you will call SRWMD at 1-800-226-1066 and request _their_ "Boat Ramp and Canoe Launch" map, they will send you a waterproof map which contains all the key information I had to leave out, at no charge.

We are working toward improving the quality and quantity of available _river_ information. If you have information you feel should be included in our next revision or a suggestion on how **Suwannee River recreation** can be improved, please drop us a line at the address in the front of this book.

Example of submissions: (and facts as of this edition)

We saw not one single bridge crossing the river, (highway **or** railroad), other than **Hwy. 136,** had any identification of any kind posted so it can be seen from the river. It still does not!

SUWANNEE RIVER STATE PARK had **"ZERO"** Park identification _at their ramp_ that can be seen **_from_** the river! For this edition, we called the park office and asked if they had corrected the problem. Their answer was "no!"

# CONTENTS

# THUMBNAIL HISTORY AND ORIGIN OF THE OKEFENOKEE, "LAND OF THE TREMBLING EARTH."

The Okefenokee Basins origin extends back in time for millions of years. It seems that the general shape of this shallow, sandy depression originated in the Pleistocene period (Ice Ages), over one million years ago. The basin was formed on a coastal terrace by changes in the level of the oceans. Sea level dropped, hesitated, sometimes for centuries, and dropped again as the last great glacial ice sheet formed in Canada, Greenland, Northern Europe, Russia, and the mountains around the world. The ice sheet captured snow and rainwater that had been falling into, or flowing into, the oceans.

It seems that the Okefenokee formed as a bay or a tidal marsh during one or more periods of sea level standstill that molded several relatively level terraces on the Atlantic Coastal plain. Over many millennia, dozens of millennia, hundreds of millennia, the landscape of the basin was shaped and reshaped. Climate changed. Temperatures rose and fell. Rainfall patterns fluctuated; ages of heavy rain, ages of draught. Sea levels rose and fell. Ancient shorelines left sandy beaches and dunes. Ancient rivers reached the sea in an ancient bay. The rivers deposited sandy bars in their deltas that developed at their mouths.

Thin deposits of limestone beneath the Okefenokee basin slowly dissolved. Small areas, often less than an acre, subsided slightly. They filled with water, then vegetation, and over the years, with peat. Large areas also sank from a foot to several feet as the lenses of limestone dissolved. These large oval areas, sometimes covering thousands of acres, are called "Carolina Bays." They formed a basin for a lake.

Prevailing winds blew across the lakes and formed sandy deposits on the southeastern rims. Over the millennia the lakes filled with peat, like other areas of the Okefenokee Basin. The ovals of some of the Carolina Bays still can be detected in parts of the Okefenokee. Differences in vegetation and crescent-shaped "islands" remain along their long-extinct edges. During the late Pleistocene, between around 35,000 and 8,000 years ago, it appears that the Okefenokee basin was a dry, sandy savanna of grassland and scattered oaks. Windblown sands probably deposited some of the sandy ridges in and around the Okefenokee during this time. The area was frequently swept by wild fire. It was not a swamp.

The earth's climate changed significantly around 18,000 years ago. The world became warmer. The last great ice sheets began to melt. The waters in the ocean rose slowly over the coastal shelf that had been exposed during the growth of the glaciers. Finally the groundwater table in the Okefenokee Basin began to rise around 8,000 years ago. Wind patterns changed. Rainfall increased. A clay bottom, in some places 400 feet thick deposited over millions of years, held the water in the basin. Soils in low areas remained wet year-round. The Okefenokee Swamp began to form.

Ever increasing rains brought nature's carpet-layers to do their jobs on the geological stage that had been prepared. Rainwater ponded. Life flourished in the lakes, then died, sank to the bottom, and began to form peat that covers the swamp. It was a carpet composed of dead mosses, ferns, grasses, sedges, lilies, and bladderworts, and many other plants and animals. This was only a moment ago in geological time. The oldest peat in the swamp is only about 7,000 years old.

The oldest radio carbon date on basal peat (peat resting on sand) is 6,600 years old. During its earliest 2,000 years, it appears that the Okefenokee Swamp was an area of scattered freshwater marshes and lakes. Peat continued to accumulate in low areas. A foot deep, two, three; until it became six to eight feet deep in many areas. The shallow valleys became marshes and ponds, the low sandy ridges became islands, covered by long leaf pine trees. The islands were separated by water during the rainy season, by peat year-round.

Then about 4,500 years ago, the landscape of the Okefenokee began to take on a new appearance. Cypress trees and other wetland species invaded the swamp. Swamp forests developed. Periodic droughts occurred. Accompanying forest fires burned small patches or swept across vast stretches of the swamp. The fires created openings for a new generation of plants. By 2,500 years ago, the Okefenokee came to look like today's swamp. This constantly changing landscape has persisted despite many natural and human disturbances.

The first **Okefenokee National Wildlife Refuge** biologist, **H. A. Carter,** recognized that the important determination of all life in the swamp is the fluctuation of water level. During much of the year the peat is covered with a few inches of water, especially in the marshy areas. When the peat decomposes, the process produces gas. This methane gas or carbon dioxide usually escapes into the atmosphere, but is occasionally trapped in pockets of peat. In the open prairies there are few deep roots to anchor the peat together. These large bubbles push the peat upward, sometimes reaching the surface of the water. These masses of peat, usually called floatants, or in the Okefenokee called "batteries," sometimes continue to float on the surface of the water covered prairies. Grasses, sedges, ferns, and small shrubs begin to grow on them and they become small peat islands.

If they continue to float, cypress trees, hollies, and heaths begin to grow on these little islands. If they survive, they become peat islands in the prairie, covered with trees. They are then no longer called batteries, they are called "houses." Some of these houses are over 700 years old. Some of them have joined together to form "timber bays." These bays eventually become cypress, bay, or gum forests. The peat floor in these houses is often covered with dead limbs, leaves, and needles. Occasionally during extended draughts, these houses, with their piles of fuel, burn. Sometimes, if the water level is very low, the fire continues to burn the peat beneath the house. When the water level rises following the draught, a lake forms in the hole in the peat where the house once stood.

Then the process of succession begins again as the lake bottom again fills with peat. So the swamp not only originated 7,000 years ago; it originated last year, last month, and yesterday. Patches of it will be born tomorrow.

## EARLY INHABITANTS

Indians first came to live in the area *around the swamp* sometime around 2,500 BC. Around 500 AD the mound-building Indians known as the "Weeden Island Culture" settled inside the Okefenokee. Some of the villages may have housed as many as several hundred people.

To the Indians, the abundant fish and wildlife must have been The Horn of Plenty. They had everything they could possibly need. Plenty of fish and game for food; the water probably was clean enough to drink from the swamp in those times. They had abundant fruits, nuts, and berries. With the abundant animals came plenty of hides for shelter and clothing. The Okefenokee must have been a beautiful and peaceful place in those days.

Evidence of many villages has been found at sites along the outer edges of the swamp. Inside the swamp, evidence of villages has been found on Chesser Island, Floyds Island, Number One Island, Bugaboo Island, Billys Island, Honey Island, Blackjack Island, Mixons Hammock, Cravens Hammock, and Hickory Hammock.

Following the Weeden Island period, the Indian population appears to have declined in the swamp, especially after 1,200 AD. Between 1750 and 1840, Seminoles began settling in the swamp, using it as a refuge. Also, around 1830, those Cherokee Indians that refused to be relocated to Oklahoma fled into the swamp. The swamp became a good hiding place.

During the summer of 1838, a small band of Indians led by Coacoochee (Wild Cat) who was called the "Napoleon of the Seminoles," also moved into the swamp. After the massacre of the Wildes family at Kettle Creek and other atrocities, Georgia Federal troops again moved back into the area. General Charles R. Floyd was in command of the Federal troops and began to put pressure on the Indians hiding in the swamp. On November 9th, 1838 General Floyd left Ft. Gilmer (near Fargo, GA) and marched to the area just outside what is now the gate of the Stephen Foster Park and built a small picket fort. He called it Fort Tatnall.

Shortly after, he and his men marched on foot to Billys Island where he built another fort. This one he named Fort Walker in honor of one of his gallant officers. Floyd later marched eight and one half hours across the swamp, with roughly 230 men, to a larger island never before seen by a whiteman. His officers named it Floyd's Island. There in a beautiful Hammock, they found 14 or 15 houses. This was the village they were seeking, but the Indians had known they were coming and had already fled. They explored the island, burned the village and marched eastward across the open ponds and prairies of the eastern swamp.

Indian camps were also found on Little Cowhouse (Chesser) Island and Cedar Hammock by army patrols. Several wagons were attacked by Indians on the east side of the swamp. A man named Mudge from Lowndes County was killed. Although it was easy to assume that Ft. Mudge near Cowhouse Island was named for this casualty, forts are usually named for army officers. Lt. R. R. Mudge of the 3rd artillery was killed at Dade's massacre on Dec. 28, 1835 and the fort was probably named in his honor.

Only one small band of Seminole warriors; elaborately dressed in their bright colored shirts; was encountered by a patrol led by Floyd's executive officer, Colonel Randolph Revill. One of the Indians in this band was killed on Nov. 25, 1841.

By 1850, the age of the Indians living in the swamp had passed. Today, only Indian mounds, pottery shards, stories and Indian names remain as a reminder of their life in the swamp.

## LOGGING IN THE OKEFENOKEE

From 1850 to 1930 there were dozens of logging companies working in the swamp at one time or another. Those more well known to historical recorders are such companies as S. F. Walker Co., The Suwannee Canal Co., Americus Manufacturing Co., Frank Snell Lumber Co., Council Lumber Co., Scott-Kendrick Lumber Co., and K-3-S Company.

The first big effort by a major logging company came in 1889. A company named the Suwannee Canal Company was formed with the idea of draining the swamp and cutting off its valuable timber. The swamp was purchased from the State of Georgia for a total of $63,000. At today's values, that would be well into the millions. The first group failed and abandoned their logging efforts around 1897. The land was transferred to the late Henry R. Jackson family in 1899 as part of the Jackson trust. In 1901 the Jackson's sold the property to a prominent lumberman from Philadelphia named Charles S. Hebard. Additional lands were purchased by Mr. Hebard in 1902 just before his untimely death later the same year. Meanwhile, several other companies tried their luck but soon also succumbed to the great difficulty and high cost of removing the timber.

## A NEW ERA IS BORN

Around 1904, Charles Hebard, Jr. and his brother, Daniel, formed what was to be the largest and most successful of all the companies, The Hebard Lumber Company of Thomas County, Georgia. However, they did not begin actual logging operations into the Okefenokee until 1909 when they leased another 219,500 acres. They formed an offshoot company called "The Hebard Cypress Company." Then, with sound financial backing, they began building their own railroad into the swamp to make it easier and less costly to get the timber to market. This began the largest of all the logging operations deep inside the Okefenokee.

The Hebard's systematically extended their logging operation across the swamp, extending south from Hopkins to Craven's Hammock in 1912 and to Pine Island and Mixons Hammock by 1915. Within a year they were cutting timber between Mixons Hammock and Minnies Island, and the railroad had been extended across Jones Island and all the way to Billys Island.

Business was so brisk that the Hebards hired a second company, called "Pine Plume Lumber Company" of Savannah, Georgia, to market their products all over the world. Then, since cypress was their main interest, they leased all rights to "Twin Tree Lumber Co. of Alabama to cut the pines from the high ground islands, such as Mitchells, Jones, Blackjack, Billys and Floyds.

By 1916, the work force of lumbermen, railroad men, equipment operators, etc. had swollen to an unusually large work force. There was a need to house the workers and their families closer to their work area. In 1917, the Hebards drew up plans for a logging camp to be located on Billys Island. The island was high ground, and was more than large enough to support their plans. Work began the same year and by 1918, Billys Island was a bustling "Boom Town."

## BILLYS ISLAND

Billys Island soon became a very large settlement. It eventually boasted a population of over 600 people. The island was divided up and laid out according to the plans. There were special areas set aside for the black and the white. Each had their own schools, churches, a *very small* sawmill for local purposes, a machine shop, hotel, several cafes, and even a theater. It was as complete as a small town of its time.

About 1919, Twin Tree Lumber Co. subleased the turpentine rights for the islands to a company named Darling Turpentine Company, who then built a turpentine still operation on Billys Island; adding more jobs and people. It continued in operation until 1921. Twin Tree Lumber continued in operation until about 1926 when it finally closed its sawmill operation in Hopkins for good.

By about 1925 most of the larger more profitable timber had been harvested by the Hebard Cypress Company and logging operations began to slow. By 1926, they abandoned their logging camp at Billys Island and moved their operation to the north end of the swamp. They established a new camp just north of Hopkins.

By late 1926 their railroad had reached almost to Dinner Pond. But the company now realized that even with the railroad, they were no longer getting enough timber to market and it was becoming unprofitable. In 1927 they closed their sawmill at Hebardville and discontinued operations for good. However, they did retain all rights to the land, and in later years leased land to smaller companies for logging up until around 1937.

After the closing of Billys Island, some families lingered on for awhile until there were only a few. The last family to leave was the Lee family. They stayed on until 1932. After a dispute with the logging company, who still held the rights to the island, they were finally evicted by the sheriff.

## MY OPINION
In those days, living in the middle of the swamp must have been harsh living. The hardships they endured just to cut the trees, wading knee to hip deep in water and mud, alligators and snakes was a daily routine. In those days, there was no such thing as a chain saw. It all had to be done with an axe, two man crosscut saws and sweat. In the summer, the only cooling they had in their small houses were open windows (which I'm sure the No-see-ums, mosquitoes and flies loved). In the winter their only heat was from fireplaces, wood stoves and kerosene heaters. Flooring in the houses had large cracks between the boards (as evidenced in the still standing Tom & Iva Chesser home on Chesser Island). Houses were of plain wood frame construction. In those days insulation was unheard of. The swamp was far more dangerous then. The alligators and snakes were more plentiful than today. As I'm sure the mosquitoes were also. It took sheer guts, sweat, strength and determination to survive in such a hostile

environment. Another difficult part of their life was that they had to transport all of their supplies from Hebardville at the far northeast corner of the swamp (near what is now Waycross, GA). However, they could get some supplies at a company store on the island and they did have access to the railroad to use for a trip to town for other supplies.

Though extremely difficult by today's standards; I envy their way of life. It was pure, simple and unspoiled in the 1920s. These were truly hard working decent country folk. I would wager; not a soul on the whole island even thought about locking their doors when they left the house. They never had to worry about someone stealing their furniture or their belongings while they were out. Marijuana and cocaine were not in their vocabulary. They probably never even heard of it. It must have been a good and pure life in that respect.

However, I was reminded by Professor Trowell that there was *plenty* of moonshine available!

## ENVIRONMENTAL DAMAGE

It's a matter of record that the Hebard Cypress Company (a) Invested $2,000,000 in their logging operation, (b) they cut and removed 425,000,000 board feet of lumber from the Okefenokee Swamp, (c) for this era, it was estimated that this amount of lumber was enough to completely build a large city of 42,000 homes, (d) the majority of the above figures was cypress. Many fine old specimens were over 400 years old. It has been estimated that all of the smaller companies put together *might* come close to matching the amount of timber Hebard Cypress removed. However, that is only speculation.

**The Okefenokee National Wildlife Refuge** was born and the park service took over complete administration of the Okefenokee Swamp in 1937. We can all be thankful for this. The Okefenokee will now remain a place for all of us, our grandchildren and their grandchildren to come and enjoy the beauty as it must have been a hundred years ago. Though the logging companies cut and removed copious amounts of timber, the swamp still retains its beauty and mystique. Today, one can boat or canoe into the swamp and see it almost as it was many years ago. Billys Island is open to the public. However, there is little left to suggest it was once a bustling and thriving community. It is visited twice daily by a park service tour boat. It is a short trip from the park office and many people come here to picnic or sightseeing.

Billys Island is a great picnic spot. Only a very short paddle form the campground. The Wildlife Service installed an excellent dock here (for their twice daily tour boat).

## WHERE THE *"DOWN THE RIVER"* IDEA STARTED —
## LEM GRIFFIS Fish Camp, 40 years ago!

In 1958, my first experience on the Suwannee River was a most memorable one. I didn't realize it at the time, but my chance meeting with a man named LEM GRIFFIS, of Fargo, Georgia, would leave me with many good memories, and later prompt me to travel the entire river by canoe. On several trips I spent days bass fishing with him in the Okefenokee swamp. I hired him to guide me in the swamp.

As I would cast, he would sit there grinning under that big floppy hat, cracking jokes or pointing out something in the trees that I had not seen. He was a talker. He should have been a comedian since he never ran out of something funny to say. We became good friends. I was not to find out until long after he had passed away that he was known all over the South for his tall yarns. He would come up with some of the most preposterous, humorous, far-fetched stories I had ever heard. His simplistic, straight faced humor was outstanding. His simple *homemade* puzzles were dumfounding; yet he never had a day of formal school in his life.

The day we first met and each time thereafter, he was dressed as he had dressed most of his life I suppose. He wore bib overalls with the legs a little too short, his feet were large and he wore no shoes. He did wear a shirt and hat. His floppy old brown hat with a wide brim looked as if he had worn it the last 30 years. (It looked just like the one Buddy Ebson wore on the Beverly Hillbillys TV show).

He was tall and thin with big ears and narrow features that where the owner of one of the biggest smiles in the state of Georgia. His eyes would get a sort of twinkle in them when he was pulling one of his usual pranks, or telling one of his famous tales. He enjoyed teasing and playing with people's mind. He would offer you several types of homemade puzzles and get you to try to work them.

He would flash a big grin when he knew he had you stumped; then very quickly he would work the puzzle. He did it so fast that you couldn't see what he had done . . . then he would put it back together quickly, grin and say . . . "thar, see how easy tiz? Now yaw'll try it again." Once again I would try only to fail. It tickled him to no end that I could not figure it out. He loved it!

Lem was a easy going born prankster with a rare gift of gab. If personality was money; he would have been a millionaire. I have serious doubts there is anyone that met him that didn't like him. One never knew what he would be up to next. Very outgoing, big smile, a razor sharp wit and dry humor is the best way I can describe him. He was the swamp model of Will Rogers.

My wife and I were talking with Lem and several of his family one day when I got another surprise. They told us that Lem had been *the* swamp consultant on the movie **"SWAMP WATER"**, staring **Walter Brennen** and **Dana Andrews.** I had seen the movie and had liked it. With a laugh, they told us Lem had gone to the Premiere of the movie and it was the *first time in his life* that he had worn shoes, and *they were large heavy brogans*. I guessed it was because of the *size* of his feet. He needed *lots* of room. When my wife and I asked him if this was true he flashed his biggest grin and said "Yep!" Remembering back, I would guess he probably would have needed at least a size 12.

I'm not certain but I think Lem only had one brother. His name was Buddy. (If he had others, I never met nor was told about them). Buddy dressed much the same as Lem, except he wore shoes and was huskier built. He wore a *huge* black felt hat *that had an extra wide* brim. But they were as different as day and night. Buddy was slightly younger than Lem, but he was very quiet and shy. He would never say much unless someone spoke to him. He seemed to prefer to just stand quietly on the sideline and watch what Lem was up to. However, I do remember seeing him smile a couple of times. He was so shy, it was a chore to get him to open up.

Lem and Buddy were raised most of their life in the swamp, but I seem to remember they were born somewhere else and moved there at a very early age. I know they had lived there most of their 60 something years. Lem knew the swamp like the back of his hand. Buddy probably did also but he never mentioned it. I believe Lem was in his late 50's or early 60's when we first met.

I had read somewhere that the swamp had superb bass fishing and I wanted to try it, so my wife and I had driven 250 miles to Fargo, GA, at the edge of the Okefenokee to fish. We came here knowing only that we wanted to fish the swamp and no idea where to go, who to see, or how to get in there.

When we arrived in Fargo, we inquired at the small grocery store in town where was the best place to go. We were told about Lem and GRIFFIS' FISH CAMP right on the edge of the swamp. It sounded exactly like what we were looking for so we headed for it. We found it had a couple of cabins, some camping spaces, a large unpainted frame house, and a tiny little building Lem called his "office and museum." There was also a good sandy place to put boats in at the river, and he had 2 fourteen foot aluminum Jon boats to rent. For a small fee Lem would take you into the swamp and show you some good places to cast for bass. I forget what he charged but it was not much at the time. About the second or third trip, we were surprised to find he had another cabin and one of the family had opened a tiny restaurant up front. But I'm getting ahead of myself.

When we arrived, he came out to meet us and I asked, "Are you Lem?" With a grin as big as a barn door he said, *"YEP, but it ain't my fault!"* I told him that I had heard he was a good fisherman and could show me where the big ones were . . . he grinned and said, *"Shore! They be so big ya gotta bring 'em back but one a time 'cause they'd be sink yore boat."* Lem agreed to guide me into the swamp and show me some good "fishin." From then on we became good friends.

View looking north – 20 ft. of high grasses on both sides.
Main canal on right.

### THE SILL

Before I move on, I would like to explain the "sill." The sill is an earthen dam roughly eight feet tall that runs north and south about 5.5 miles along the Southwestern edge of the swamp. There are two large concrete spillways near the southern most part of the sill. Its purpose is to maintain a constant water level in the swamp to keep down fires. At the time of my trips with Lem, I think there was only one double spillway (I don't remember seeing another) and it was approachable by boat from the river side. The water spilling over becomes the Suwannee River. **(Author's note: There is currently a proposal on the table from the Corps of Engineers and the Park Service to breach this sill. It is my opinion that if this happens - canoeing in the south swamp will be gone forever.)** The first couple of trips, the flow of water was just enough that when Lem gunned his motor into the spillway, we went up and over. I was surprised. I never would have thought it possible.

When I saw what he was about to do, I expected the bow of the Jon boat to bury itself in the oncoming water and we would be swamped. Much to my surprise, we went up and over with ease. Today, the sill spillway looks much different. It now has multiple spillways and railings all the way across so I don't think it would be possible to do this any more.

Back to the story . . .
It was either the second or third time I had come to fish. One morning we were fishing somewhere east of the sill and the fishing was slow. Lem says to me, *"Wanna see a big gator?"* I said, *"Sure."* I expected to see something around 6 or 8 feet. He cranked up and we went a short ways farther to the East then turned north into a small waterway that looked like a creek. As he shut off the motor and picked up his paddle he said, *"Now be reel quiet, when we round this h'yar next bend, look to yore right, up on thet bank and you'll see 'em."* He paddled very slow and quiet . . . then suddenly as we rounded the bend, I got the shock of my life! <u>He was right</u>, up there on that bank hardly 30 yards from us was a **_HUGE 'gator_** that looked like a prehistoric monster. That ole guy must have been well over 50 years old.

We were in Lem's 14-foot Jon boat and that gator looked like it would have hung over both the bow and the stern. His back was as broad as a horse and a belly that looked like he had just swallowed one. When he spotted us he hit the water like a locomotive that had just fallen from a railroad trestle. He made waves that were big enough I thought it would splash water into our boat. I let out a war hoop **"Oh my God!"** and was frozen with fear.

Lem grinned from ear to ear and said quite matter of factly, *"Big 'un, ain't he?"* I could tell by the grin on his face that we weren't in any immediate danger. He got a big charge out of scaring heck out of me.

To be polite, all I'll say here is, "It's a darn good thing I had gone to the bathroom before we left camp!" The only other gator I have ever seen to this day that was even close to that guy's size was stuffed in **Ross Allen's** exhibit at Silver Springs, Florida around 1962. It looked like a young railroad box car. I don't remember for sure but I think it was 15 foot something. We went back to our fishing and caught a couple more later that afternoon.

On my next trip to Lem's place he was booked. He assured me I wouldn't get lost if I went into the swamp alone. So I rented his boat and motor, tried his _jump_ over the sill flow, and had no trouble. I tried the same spots we had fished before but Lem must have been my luck as I only caught a couple mud fish. On the next trip, my wife and I were discussing camping in the swamp but Lem told us it was against the law to be inside the park boundaries after dusk. He said we should camp on the small sandbar outside the boundary. As we were leaving, I went to fill an extra jug with water. Lem asked "what's that fer?" I told him for coffee. He said with a big grin, _"what ya'll need thet fer? Thet river water makes tha best dang coffee in tha world!"_ I thought about it and agreed it probably would do just fine since we had a percolator. We took his advice and camping on the small sandbar just outside the swamp boundary, also trying his "river water" coffee since it would be boiled anyway. Not bad!

We spent an enjoyable day fishing, cruising the river and this was our first night camping. My wife and I were young at the time and were not very experienced campers nor were we well equipped. I built a large lean to, using branches and leaves with a couple heavy blankets over fresh leaves for a mattress. After supper we were enjoying the quiet and peaceful evening just as the sun went down. There was still a little light in the sky, and the air was still when _I thought_ . . . I heard _wings._ (I have been informed by knowledgeable bird watchers that owls have silent wings but I still believe it was the sound that caught my attention — however, it _could_ have been the movement).

I looked up just in time to see a monstrous owl light in a dead treetop across the river from our camp. His horns were visible since he was silhouetted against the sky. He must have been **the granddaddy of all owls.** He looked like a 30-gal. drum with wings. I approximated his wingspan (by the tree and limbs the following morning) to have had at least a six or seven foot wingspan if it was an inch. My wife and I were awed by his size and didn't move a muscle. As he called with a deep authoritative voice, I decided to answer him. It was amusing to watch him crane his neck trying to locate that _"cute little thing"_ who was answering his call to come and play. After a dozen or so calls, he came over to our side and lit in a tree near our campsite to get a closer look. It wasn't long before he discovered our trickery and left in disgust. To this day, in all my 69 years, I have never seen _any_ owl that would come even close to that fellows size. Giant owls, Giant gators, they _grow 'em big_ in that swamp!

We have just turned in and were almost asleep when we heard a pig on the other side of the river scream as if he were mortally wounded. My wife, scared half out of her wits clung to me as if she was afraid I would leave her. She kept saying, "what was that." I said I had no idea as we strained our ears for more sounds in the dark; only to hear the pig scream again and again several seconds apart. It seemed like each time he screamed, he was farther away. Needless to say, we didn't sleep very well the rest of the night.

The next morning we headed for Lem's. We told him about the screaming pig and he laughed and said, "Oh, I fergot to tell y'all thet we ketched an ole bear across frum where y'all be camped, jest last week." With another big grin he said, "He wuz a litlun tho, mabe three 'r' four hunert pounds. Y'all probly heered an ole bear that ketched a pig." I saw my wife's eyebrows go up but she didn't say anything and I let it drop. I heard about it later though. So off we went for some more fishing. The fishing turned out to be poor that morning so we decided to return to camp early for lunch.

Too late! Wild pigs had gotten into our camp and had totally destroyed everything we had except our canned goods. Even the labels on most of those were gone so we had no idea what they contained. They even opened and cleaned out our cooler. By that time my wife had had enough. Sadly, we packed up and headed for home. As we were about to pull out, Lem laughed and said, "Y'all ain't gonna let them lil ole pigs bother ya are ya?" We laughed and said, "no, but all our food is gone and I don't want to have to go into town for more, so we'll see you next trip." Lem hadn't bothered to warn us about the wild pigs, and being new to this area _and_ green campers, we learned a lesson.

We returned to see Lem a couple more times before I left Florida, but those times we "chickened out" and stayed in one of his rustic cabins. It was during these trips, listening to Lem's stories and fishing the upper Suwannee, that it occurred to me how wonderful it would be to just float down the river fishing and camping all the way to the Gulf. That was 40 years ago.

I heard later that Buddy passed away first, then Lem, I believe in the late 60's. Meanwhile, I had moved out of state and didn't return until Dec., 1992 and retired Feb., 1993.

I have been back a couple of times and visited with Lem's son, Arden who still lives on the old place and now has only campsites. The big house and "museum" are long gone, and the little restaurant up front has long ago been closed. I have fond memories of this place and Lem and Buddy. They were fine people.

### THE DECISION TO DO IT!

In 1995, I saw Marla Weechs' (of **WFTV** Channel 9 Orlando) *"Florida – by Paddle, Pack, & Pedal,"* part of which was canoeing Florida rivers. That clinched it. I made my decision! I again got the urge to canoe down the Suwannee River. Expecting to go alone, I bought a clean square stern aluminum canoe and a 3 HP Johnson, (for emergency use). I now had lots of time and was *itching to go down that river!*

I spent the rest of the year getting everything ready. Along about Jan. of 1996, I began posting messages on CompuServ looking for retirees to go along on the trip but to no avail. By early February, I still had no one interested so I resigned myself to the fact I was going to make the trip alone.

As a last minute thought, I called Milt Salamon of the FLORIDA TODAY NEWS, the newspaper in Brevard County, Florida, to ask how I could post some sort of message in the paper looking for others to go along on the trip. Milt was out so I was switched to **BILL SARGENT,** the OUTDOORS editor. He listened intently as I told him what I was planning on doing and that I would like some company. He said, "That's no problem, let me do a little story on it and we'll see if we can find you some canoers." I gave him the particulars and he ran a great story in his column. He followed up two weeks later with a second story. That put everything in motion.

I was *overwhelmed* with callers. Twenty-eight I believe! Most, but not all, were retirees and . . . _ALL_ said the exact same thing. *"I've wanted to canoe down that darn river for over 20 years!"* . . . Suddenly, I had company.

Twelve people attended our first meeting. All wanted to go. We had our second meeting about a month later, and only eight showed up. When it was time to leave on our preliminary *test run to the Okefenokee,* only **three** were available. So the four of us took a short trip into the swamp at Stephen Foster Recreational Park to check out our video camera setup and other equipment.

## FIRST TEST RUN

I had spent months getting my canoe ready. I redid the inside with chromate to eliminate glare and future corrosion; had special rain covers made; made a "lattice" deck insert to keep my gear up off the hull in case of rain, etc.; backs for the seats; and too many other chores to mention. Most of my camping equipment *was still fresh* from a trip I had made to Boundary Waters of Northern Minnesota, July of the previous year so I didn't have to do much to it.

The main reason for going on our test run was to check the video camera *mount* I had made for the bow of the canoe. Though it looked good on the canoe, I had never tested it. It was an aluminum plate on 10" legs with the camera mounted directly above the bow. I also made a rain cover and anti-glare plates; it looked and worked great *(at home!).*

March 14th, we pulled out about 8 AM from Cocoa and headed north. We had not been to any of the locations where we would eventually pull out on the Suwannee so our first stop was BRANFORD, FL. which would be our second pull out. We discovered there was no place to camp at the pull out so we spoke with **Gene Broome,** the owner of **THE DIVE CENTER,** and got permission to camp on his property when we arrived. We next moved on to the **"SPIRIT OF THE SUWANNEE" Campground,** just north of LIVE OAK (which would be our first pullout). We were delighted to find the campground was extremely nice and had everything we needed and then some. After checking out the downtown area to see where we could re-supply, we moved on to Fargo, GA which would be our put in point. We didn't worry that it was getting late in the evening since we had reservations. (To stay at a Stephen Foster Rec. Park campsite, one must call ahead for reservations – their 800 number is listed in the back.)

We called ahead telling them we would be late arriving and were told *"we close the office at 6 PM,* but no problem, your campsite will be *posted* on the board at the office." We arrived after dark, picked up our site number and headed for the site *only to find someone else in it.* By this time we were so tired we just found another site and put down. After a quick supper, we crashed.

In 50+ years of camping under all kinds of conditions, I knew better than to leave any food out on the table. I knew there would be "critters" in the night. However, thinking it would be nothing like "bear country" camping (no dangerous animals), I foolishly put our food supplies inside our tent. Everything was about 2 feet inside the tent and at least a foot from the wall.

About 2 AM I was *awakened by a noise* that sounded like something trying to get in. I turned on my flashlight and saw nothing. I was just lying back down when I heard paper rustling outside the door. What the heck is that, I thought. I unzipped the tent fly and shined my light right into the face of an unconcerned 'coon that could have played right tackle for the Green Bay Packers, about two feet from my tent fly, and feasting on our bread. By now the others were awake. I said to them, "I thought we brought all of the supplies inside." All chimed in and said *"they **were** brought in."* Fearfully I shined my light around — sure enough, my fears were well founded.

That fatso had cut a 12" gash in my new tent wall and had helped himself. At first, I wanted to do him in . . . but I thought better of it since it was *MY fault* for leaving it where he could get to it . . . not his! So I left him to gorge himself and went back to bed with a disgusted feeling. Next morning we gave the tent a new stylish look. It now sported a **big** red X inside and out, covering the ripped area (red H/D duct tape). It still has it today as a reminder to never again put food inside my tent, even if there are no bears around.

After scrounging breakfast, we headed for the launch ramp, signed out at the office, mounted the camcorder on the bow of the canoe, and we were on our way. The water was still, the sky was a stunning blue with little white puffy clouds here and there. The birds were singing and there were no mosquitoes. What more could a guy ask for. It was a beautiful morning.

We began shooting right after we left the short canal from the marina to the lake. We had not gone more than a couple hundred yards down lake when we saw a large 'gator that looked around 10 feet long, resting draped over a log at the edge of the water. Since the camera was fixed mounted, I had to point the canoe at what I wanted to film.

A ten foot 'gator rests on a log. He was the largest one we saw on this trip. There were hundreds of smaller ones. A few would let you get close for a picture but not all.

The camcorder malfunctioned and we didn't get him. After a few anxious moments we figured out what caused the problem and off again we went. Down lake and about a dozen 'gators later, we turned north into the creek that is the main **canoe trail** north and headed for *Minnie's Lake* roughly 5 or 6 miles into the swamp. (The canoe trail is well marked.)

The scenery was absolutely beautiful. We wound our way upstream, against a slight current, photographing everything that moved, and a lot that didn't, and several dozen 'gators mostly 4 to 5 footers. By 2 PM the sun had changed and the lighting wasn't what I wanted so we headed back to camp. I should mention that on this trip in and back, we passed several Jon boats with fishermen, and at least four or five canoes. I mention this so the person who has never been into the swamp will feel comfortable knowing there is enough traffic that they don't have to worry about getting lost. Also, the canoe trail is well marked. I apologize for repeating myself here, but I think it important. There is little danger here in this swamp; if you use common sense. In other words . . . don't be foolish enough to get too close to the 'gators, etc. Also, in all of our time spent in the swamp (both trips), we did not see a single snake. I'm sure they were around, but stay in your canoe or keep to the regular paths (on Billys Island). I doubt you will see any either. But it is possible. They are there so stay alert.

Next morning, we went out filming until around noon. The wind came up enough that we lost the reflections so we headed in early. We relaxed and worked on equipment for the balance of the day and the following morning we headed for home. I couldn't wait to see what we had on film. Though my camera had a playback mode to check the film shot, it is black and white only; and I wanted to see it in color.

When I finally got to see the swamp film, it was super. However, I wasn't satisfied with the slight side "motion" we got as the paddle stroked. It was very slight, but it was noticeable. Though other people who saw it said they liked it because it gave them the feeling they were in the canoe with us . . . I decided to go back and do it again, only this time hand held so I could compare the two. I didn't want to film our long trip down river with second rate camera work. My wife jokingly accused me of just looking for an excuse to go back to the swamp. I gave her Lem's grin and said "Yep!"

## SECOND OKEFENOKEE TEST RUN

Those who went on the first trip were now busy and couldn't go, so I called Randy, who was to be my paddler when we went down the Suwannee. He said he would gladly go with me. However, he had _never_ had a camcorder in his hand before in his life, so I had to go over everything with him from the beginning. He needed to know how to operate the camera since he would be in front of the canoe.

We found a good campsite and setup camp right away so we would have time to roam around the area looking for wildlife. Late that evening, we got superb close-up footage of a beautiful adult gray fox who paid no attention whatsoever to us filming.

The next morning early as we headed for the launch ramp, right next to our campsite were four deer. Then a little over 100 feet more we discovered a 6 foot 'gator right inside the camp, laying quietly in the drainage ditch next to the main road. We remarked that he was probably looking for an easy dog or 'coon meal.

After we were satisfied we wouldn't get any more wildlife shots, we loaded up and headed for the main lake. For the rest of the day, Randy did the shooting, I did the 'directing,' how, what, and where to shoot. Randy learned quickly and we were off re-tracing the steps of our last test run.

We spent most of the day filming and returned to camp around three. I had told Randy about the 'coons coming into camp and that these guys were the "city slickers" of the woods. They were expert in knowing where to find food in this campground; and would get into everything, food or anything else.

We were just talking about 'coons and planning to set up to get footage of them that night, when up struts a bold, fat young 'coon, right into our campsite. He didn't seem to mind that it was still early in the day. He was hungry and didn't give a darn if we saw him or not. I grabbed the camcorder as he sauntered into camp and climbed inside our van (the side door was open). We watched him as he carefully checked everything out. After he was satisfied there was nothing there of interest, he climbed out, looked us over and sauntered off as nonchalant as though he owned the campground.

We got some great footage. Later that evening, we scrubbed a piece of pepperoni around on the table, left some crumbs and waited for them to show. They didn't let us down. The sun had just gone down when a huge pair of adult 'coons showed up. They were on the table in a flash. The first one there trying to keep the other one from coming up with snarls and growls. We enjoyed watching them and got some interesting footage.

After reviewing both tapes of the swamp, I didn't want to risk getting film that wouldn't be perfect, so I removed the *bow mount* and opted to shoot the whole trip down river entirely hand held. It turned out to be the best choice though it was a pain in the rear for Randy since he had to keep the camera bag up front under his feet and it left him cramped with very little room. The swamp test run turned out to be a *very worthwhile trip*; as we fine tuned our needs and learned from it.

By April 1st, we were back to seven people plus myself. I wrote, and personally spoke with just about everybody I could to get good river information. One fellow on *CompuServ* suggested I contact the Suwannee River Water Management District office for river information, which I did. That was a good lead. With their information, I was able to determine the exact date I wanted to start the trip. I opted for April 17th, since I needed to have the best water possible for campsites (sandbars) as well as the temperature and bugs would not be bad at that time of year. For one reason or another, those who were so eager to go at the very beginning, found reasons why they couldn't. By the time we were ready to leave, we were down to five people and myself. **Ron Bussendorf, Randy Pieper, Harry McDonald, Ray De Fillips, and O. Van Orman.**

As it worked out . . . it could not have been a more perfect time, the size of the group was just right. Though the water was higher than we had anticipated due to bad weather in south Georgia (they had 8 inches of rain in 48 hours the week before we arrived). However, since we were now locked in, we went for it. The water level didn't bother us and the weather couldn't have been better if we had requisitioned it. I had gone to Fargo again the week before and found that the water was up so high that we couldn't see the sandbar we had planned on camping on the first night before we were to launch. So I called **Winston Peterson,** the local sheriff in Fargo, and explained our situation and asked to camp in the picnic area next to the river for that first night.

He said "OK," and we were over our first hurdle. On **April 17th,** we left Brevard County early and headed north on Highway 95 agreeing to meet at the **"SPIRIT OF THE SUWANNEE"** Campground, 4 miles north of Live Oak, Florida. We had contracted with David and Debbie Pharr, the owners of the **CANOE OUTPOST**, to leave our cars at their place. They would transport us, our canoes and equipment to our launch site at Fargo, GA, then pick us up at our pull-out point.

We had planned it so that when we pulled out after completing the first leg of the trip, we would have use of our vehicles _there_ to re-supply, wash clothes and run into town, etc. It worked out perfectly, and we didn't have to worry about the safety of our vehicles while we were on the river.

They have a large parking area next to the ramp and office (by the river), so it was not only safe, it was handy. David and Debbie will rent you as many canoes as you need and completely outfit you for a trip; whether a short or a long one, transport you to your launch point and pick you up.

### START OF THE SUWANNEE RIVER TRIP!

We arrived at the CANOE OUTPOST and the "SPIRIT OF THE SUWANNEE" Campground at about 1:45 PM. Harry and Ray were already there and loaded. David, the owner of the OUTPOST has several large vans and canoe trailers and can transport eight to ten canoes per load, including equipment and passengers. Around 3 PM we finally got everything and everyone loaded in the vans and pulled out for Fargo.

It was now a little after 4 PM. Again, our original plan was to unload and camp on the huge sandbar near the bridge; but with the water being 5 feet above normal, we had to change our plans. So we unloaded everything into the small picnic area.

Hastily unloading in the picnic area, we put everything into one big pile.
It took quite awhile to get it all sorted out.

We quickly turned to the task of sorting out the *giant pile* of equipment, fixing supper and setting up tents for the night. For a short time after supper we all sat around a small fire swapping sea stories then went to bed early. We were tired and wanted to get plenty of rest for the big day ahead. At least that was what we *thought* we were going to do. **WRONG!** There were about a dozen young fellows drinking beer and partying down at the river's edge and they partied late. We knew *they* were there. What we didn't know however was that *logging trucks* would pass about every 10 or 15 minutes, and they would run up to midnight *(the highway was less than 100 feet away)*; and that there was **also** a *busy* railroad track less than half a block north of us. Before dawn, a dozen fast freights had rumbled past, all blasting their horns as if it were their last chance and wanting to get in a good one.

### THE FIRST DAY . . . Thursday, April 18th

Just as dawn was breaking we crawled out of our sleeping bags and began the task of finding breakfast and breaking camp. Some made their own, but a couple of us headed for the small restaurant located **in the rear** of the CITGO STATION, only a block north of us. (Also to make use of their restroom since there were no facilities in the park.) We had an **excellent** breakfast and the prices were reasonable. The lady who owns the place, **Lorraine,** was also very informative and helpful. **Update:** They have now closed this restaurant. But there is another . . . first building north.

After everyone had repacked their gear, we slowly began moving our canoes and equipment the 200 feet or so down to the river's edge. Four canoes and equipment took the 6 of us over an hour to move and load everything.

Finally, about 9 AM we were ready to pull out . . . at least _we thought_ we were. Van was the first one in the water and pulled out a short distance to wait for the rest of us when he yelled out "Holy @*$% . . . I've got a leak!"

Though it was serious, we made light of it and gave him a good ribbing. He had a grin on his face but it was obvious he was a bit worried. We quickly unloaded his canoe and turned it upside down for inspection. We discovered that his canoe had 4 holes in it where corrosion had eaten through. (He had borrowed it for the trip.) From then on, because of his patches and a feather in his hat, he became **"Apache Chief."**

Fortunately I had brought along some special aerospace type duct tape and Permatex for just such an emergency. We first filled the holes with Permatex, then covered them with the tape. (Despite a lot of abuse, they held up all 16 days and 213 miles of the trip.)

Shortly, we had him back in the water. After a short test run, he was satisfied that the tape would hold. At **10 AM** we formed up and headed down the river on the first leg of our trip. The temperature was comfortable in the mid 60's. The water level was above normal so the flow was strong. We paddled leisurely most of the day.

The upper river is narrow and winding and the trees and brush are solid along the banks from just below Fargo until after you get across the Florida line. Then it opens up more. We saw no pull outs on this stretch of the river. Also everything is posted.

After a short discussion we decided to find a campsite and put down early. About 4:15 PM we found a nice campsite *on the **left side*** just before the river makes a left turn. (We didn't know it at the time, but after checking maps later, I believe it was just over the state line and about where "Toms Creek" comes in.)

Before we set up camp at that location, the rest of the crew waited as Randy and I fired up our tiny little outboard and went a mile or so downstream to see if there was a better site. Nothing looked as good as this one so we decided to stay put. (I had brought the Johnson 3HP along for such extra excursions.) For the most part it was just along for the ride. Later it proved to be well worth the inconvenience and an excellent decision.

Our campsite had a *tiny* cove back in the trees that was perfect for beaching our canoes. Probably, at normal water this cove would not be as pronounced (and might not even exist). The campsite had plenty of room for 5 or 6 tents. Judging from the campfire ring, it had been used many times before.

We estimated we had traveled about 14 miles from Fargo. This particular piece of property did not have the familiar "POSTED" signs we had seen all down river on both sides. After getting our tents up, Harry and Ray broke out what became their <u>*evening ritual*</u> for the rest of the trip . . . one cold beverage before supper. We had an excellent supper and sat around a large fire for an hour or two discussing the day's events, especially Van's leaky canoe, telling jokes and sea stories. We

Roughly 14 miles from Fargo, we found a nice campsite on the left that was not posted. Plenty of room and had been used before. "About" where Tom's Creek comes in.

were all tired from our first day of paddling and with a full stomach . . . we turned in early. Van was the only one who preferred to sleep out without a tent.

With no beer parties nearby . . . no logging trucks . . . no trains . . . we all slept like babies. There were a few mosquitoes . . . but they were light and not bothersome at all. We had come prepared however; and used repellent.

### SECOND DAY . . . Friday, April 18th
We were up as the sky was just beginning to lighten. We accused Van of sleeping outdoors and not using a tent because the tent couldn't hold up under the stress of the vibrations of his snoring. We all had a good heehaw and he along with us. After a light breakfast, we broke camp. We spent considerable time on this first morning, rearranging and organizing every-thing, leisurely getting on the water a little *before nine.* We paddled slowly, slightly better than the flow of the river. It turned out that we made the whole trip at that speed since we were not in any hurry. As before, we stopped on little sandy

beaches here and there to stretch and to have lunch. There are plenty of these little sandbars along the river's edge where one can camp or just get out and stretch along this section of the river. There had been almost none on the first day's run and there had been "POSTED" signs *everywhere.*

*Note:* Though the first part of the trip (13 miles or so in Georgia) was interesting, it was not near as pretty as it became soon after we entered Florida. It seemed like the river banks

We stop for lunch and enjoy one of the sandbars along the way. There are many and come in all sizes. This was a small one. Left to right: Van, Randy, Myself, Ron and Harry.

changed . . . and we began to see sandbars. We saw no sandbars in Georgia after leaving Fargo.

We arrived at the **Hwy. 6 bridge** at exactly **2 PM.** The bridge is **20.8** miles from Fargo and we had only paddled from **10 AM till 4 PM** on the first day (6 hours). We had been on the water today only 5 hours. With roughly 45 minutes for lunch and a couple stretch breaks of 15-20 minutes each day, that meant we were averaging slightly over 2.5 miles an hour. We didn't mind since we were just starting the trip and had intended for it to be leisurely.

For future reference we stopped to check out the campsite area on the right at the bridge; and found it to be quite good.

On this side of the bridge, there is a small beach that will handle 6 or 8 canoes with ample room for tents above. We saw no other place to camp close to this location. We later learned that this is the beginning of the **"STATE CANOE TRAIL."** I might mention that the river appeared to be moving more rapidly at this point. We left this area about **2:20** and continued on. After a couple of rest stops; we put down for the night about **4:30** on a small sandy strip along the right side; roughly 5 or 6 miles south of the bridge. We had to camp high up on a bank in a small area with little room. We estimated we had traveled roughly another 12-14 miles. Again the mosquitoes were not bad at all. The weather was still cool at night and I'm sure that helped keep them down. We had zero "No-see-ums" . . . What a blessing! There was ample firewood and the area looked as if it had been used by campers before.

### THIRD DAY . . . Saturday, April 19th

Again, we were up just as the sky was getting light. By the time we ate and broke camp, it was **8 AM** exactly when we pushed off. There was a light steam coming up off the water and as the sun hit it from the side, it was a *beautiful sight.* Though we had seen 'coon tracks everywhere on the beach last evening, we did not have a single visitor in the night. As we were paddling that morning, we again teased Van that it was his snoring *that kept the "critters" away.* We all had a good laugh. About a mile downstream *as we rounded a right bend,* we discovered a fantastic campsite on the right. It was clean, sandy and flat. I had an excellent sandy pull out that could handle 6 or 8 canoes. We wished we had known it was there last evening. This campsite is back behind a huge cypress tree with *lots of exposed roots and knees.* The trees are very easy to spot. The campsite itself can't be seen easily until you're right on top of it coming around the bend (see photo next page).

A second tree about 15' downstream and not as large, sticks well out over the water *almost horizontally.* However, high river recently could make it look different so if you wish to use this site, *stay alert* or you could miss it.

About **9 AM** we passed the **Cone Bridge** launch site. It is **32.5 miles from Fargo.** That put us 12.5 miles downstream from Hwy. 6 bridge. We had covered that in only 3.5 hours on the water, for an average of 3.8 MPH. The river again appeared to have picked up speed on this area.

A very nice little campsite we found the next morning after spending the night in a poor one. It's on the right about 7-8 miles below Hwy. 6 bridge. Easy to pass it up if not alert.

### BIG SHOALS — A WORD OF **CAUTION!**

At the time of our trip, the **Shoals warning sign** (on the left up high in the trees) was in _terrible disrepair_ and difficult to read. If one is not paying close attention and misses this sign, they could quickly get into fast water. The rapids _are audible_ as you get close (depending on water level). There is no identification of any kind **at the pullout.** I would like to see a very conspicuous sign posted here.

### ONE OTHER WORD OF CAUTION!

If you are not an _experienced_ <u>swift water</u> canoer, I _highly recommend_ you _DO NOT_ attempt to run these shoals. Especially at high water. And **_certainly not_** if you have a heavily loaded canoe. However, if you are determined to go for it, the **SAFEST** place to do so is just off the right bank. About 5 miles downstream, we found some poor fellow's pack _and_ sleeping bag floating partially submerged in mid river. Nothing was salvageable. I'm sure his trip was also terminated on the spot.

Be smart! — Play it safe! **PORTAGE!**

**BIG SHOALS AT HIGH WATER**
They look like an easy run but can fool you. Sharp jagged rocks just under
the surface make them *quite* dangerous. Do not underestimate the danger here.

## BIG SHOALS RAPIDS

We arrived at the BIG SHOALS pull out about **12:30 PM** (on left side). The area where one lands their canoe is slightly difficult. There isn't enough room for more than two or three canoes at a time. Where you pull out is a sloping, slightly rocky bank, and it's difficult to tie up since the current is moving quite rapidly just a few feet out from this point. Someone had placed a rope hand line along the left edge to make it easier to hold on while trying to get in. After getting all of our canoes and gear up the bank, we walked down to the south end to check out the campsite and the launch area. We returned and ate lunch at the pullout before beginning the task of portaging everything to the campsite. Also, the trail is wide and clean so it is easy to negotiate. The campsite at the south end of the portage is excellent. It is about 20 feet above the shoals, and about 50 feet downstream of them.

It is large enough for at least 4 or 5 tents; in trees, and is *clean* and flat. It took us a little over an hour to move all four of our canoes and gear into the campsite. Lucky for us we had arrived early. At least 6 other groups later came through camp. There are other much smaller sites below but they are not nearly as nice as the main one.

It's not only an **easy** portage, it's a very pretty area. Take your time and enjoy it.

## THE PORTAGE

We had been in our campsite less than 30 minutes when we notice a "Fish and Game" plane circling tightly six or eight times directly over us and just barely clearing the tree tops.

Momentarily we stopped and watched him circle and wondered why. We figured it must be that they were just checking the campsite to see who was there.

About 30 min. after the plane left, we found out why! Ron had just finished setting up his tent and putting his gear inside when out of the brush came a Fish and Game Officer. We thought maybe we had done something wrong . . . then . . . we got bad news. The officer told us they had been looking for us since 8 AM that morning. The reason was that Ron's ex-wife had passed away. Though it was his ex – she was the mother of his children and he was in shock. It came as a shock to all of us so we told Ron to take off, that we'd take care of his canoe and gear for him. He and the officer immediately disappeared into the woods on foot. We assumed that they had a 4-wheel drive somewhere in the woods close by. We packed and stowed Ron's gear right away.

We were just settling down to catch our breath when suddenly a mixed group of a dozen or so college kids appeared. We had a brief conversation and they went on their way. About 20 minutes later, here comes another group, and then a few minutes later another, and another, and another . . . we thought we had camped in Grand Central Station. Most were hikers but a couple were canoe groups. It was a great site . . .

and we were glad we had arrived early enough to have gotten into it. We were tired but comfortable so we didn't mind the traffic. A few of them stopped to chat after enjoying the view of the rapids. Some of them were *"quite interesting"* in their tight shorts and halters! (grin)

Just about dark a group of 11 *very young* boys and two older teenagers came through camp. They were some sort of Sheriff's boy's group (probably something like Outreach) and were canoeing down river. We talked for a short while and found that they were going almost as far down river as we were, to Manatee Springs 180 miles!

We commented "that's a _very long_ trip for boys so young." Most looked to be about ten or eleven, the older boys might have been sixteen or seventeen. We watched as they brought their canoes and supplies through camp. We later walked down to the launch area to watch them put in. We were surprised to see two of the boys swim the swift current to a sandy beach on the other side. We didn't think it possible; especially being so young, but they made it.

The water at that point was far enough below the rapids that it was not as turbulent, though the current was still quite strong. We watched the others launch and paddle across to their campsite; mainly to see how they went about launching down the steep and slick embankment into swift water. Due to the lack of area to pull the canoe along side the bank and then load, they loaded the canoe first. Then put it in and lined it downstream about twenty feet to a tree trunk that stuck out; then got in from there.

Their teamwork was exceptional. We looked at each other; grinned and said, "Well I'll be darned." We were amazed they had done so well. They worked together like old pros.

Having had a tiring day, portaging, setting up camp, etc., we were beat so we ate a light supper and turned in early. Camped next to the rapids, the melodious roar of the fast rushing water tumbling over the rocks was soothing and almost hypnotizing. We sank into deep sleep almost immediately. What a _wonderful_ sound! And no mosquitoes!

From the campsite to the launch, (only about a 100 feet or so) was a little tight and muddy, but the rest of the trail was wide, dry and clean.

### FOURTH DAY . . . Sunday, April 20th

Again, up just as the first light was appearing in the sky, we took our time; had breakfast and broke camp. We had to move all of our canoes and gear another 100 feet or so down the trail to the launch site, then we had to load <u>before</u> launching. That took about 45 minutes.

The campsite is close to the launch site, however, from the edge of the campsite to the launch site is a narrow and slick path that gradually drops about 10 feet.

With several people working together, it really was not much of a chore moving everything to the launch site.

34

Since there was fast moving water, there was no way to load the canoes after putting them in so we loaded them first, launched and lined them downstream 20', then got in.

The bank we had to launch from was mostly limestone with some slick hard clay spots, steep, and approximately 7 feet above fast moving water. This looked like it would be a real tricky proposition. Surprisingly it turned out to be much easier than it looked. It was not a problem at all.

Though it looked scary at first, it turned out to be "a piece of cake." We had no problem whatsoever putting in, except for Randy's sore behind; from checking out a slick spot.

Though we had been well prepared for a mishap, every-thing went smoothly except Randy found out how slick the wet clay was near the water's edge and had a sore bottom for the rest of the day. We pulled away from our launch site below the rapids at **9:30 AM.** Randy and I took Ron's loaded canoe in tow, tying it in close so it wouldn't yaw. Surprisingly, it turned out to be no trouble at all since we were traveling most of the way with good current and with relatively little wind. Actually, it worked out well for all of us since we were able to use it to carry all of our excess items. (Like trash bags, etc.)

A few miles downstream, we found the packs and sleeping bag (mentioned earlier) floating just under the surface of the river. Undoubtedly, some person *had not heeded the warning* and tried to run the rapids loaded. Though we found his ruined gear, we wondered what had happened to <u>him</u>. Take a lesson from this, your gear should be well secured in your canoe when you are expecting to **run** fast water. Carry some parachute cord. It works great, extra strong, light, takes up no room, and it's inexpensive.

After paddling 3-4 hours, we stop on a beautiful sandbar for a "Pepperoni Break." Pepperoni keeps very well and makes a great snack with Ritz crackers.

About an hour after launching; we had some sort of *big* fish come flying out of the water next to one of our canoes. I only heard it but the others saw it. We were startled and had no idea what it was.

It became routine to make 15 to 20 minute sandbar stretch stops now and then and we usually took roughly **30 minutes** for lunch before moving on.

Around **2 PM,** we began to hear small children yelling, playing somewhere ahead of us. Shortly, we saw there was a group of about eight young kids playing at the river's edge on a tight right bend in the river. All were girls but two. We could see a station wagon sitting high up on a bluff on the south side. However, we couldn't see any *adults* anywhere.

As we were a hundred feet or so from them, the older kids decided to swim across. Several of the younger kids decided to follow. All made it across OK except for one little boy. God must have been watching. When he reached the middle of the river, he began flailing his arms and screaming. I and the others had already passed the kids except for Harry and Ray who had been lagging behind. It was a blessing that they were, for this little boy (who looked to be about seven or eight) had reached the middle and found he was unable to continue; the current in the bend was too much for him; he was nearly exhausted. If Harry and Ray had not been only a few paddle strokes away at that moment, he probably would have lost his life. They got to him just in time; had him to hang onto the side of the canoe, and paddled him safely to the shore from where the kids had started. What was strange is that no adult *ever* came down to the river to see what was going on. Harry passed the boy to a young girl who appeared to be about fifteen or sixteen years old. Though she scolded the boy for not obeying her . . . she said nothing about where the parents were. That evening we wondered if the kids had snuck off to the river and what would have happened if our guys had not been on the spot at that exact moment. Harry and Ray were understandably proud that they had been there at the right time and had done their **"Boy Scout deed for the day."** It was our main topic of discussion during supper and we were pleased things had worked out so well.

Along about **3:30 PM** we began looking for a place to put down for the night. As we rounded a small bend to the right, on the right side, we saw a small sandy beach with what looked like a little *"cubby hole"* in the back. It looked worth investigating so we stopped to check it out. There is a gully that looks like it had been a creek opening at one time. As we walked back in, there was a nice but small campsite. Barely room enough for three or four tents but it was adequate so we stopped for the night. We estimated this site to be roughly halfway between the shoals and Hwy. 75. After supper, we found a flat up higher that could hold several tents if needed.

First we did a little fishing then decided to get a bath and wash a few clothes. I was in my birthday suit bathing when a boat came flying around the bend upstream, loaded with people. I ran like heck up the bank and hid behind a tree until they were gone. I had just returned to the river when here they came again, only _this_ time . . . floating backwards; down river out of gas. I had to continue hiding behind the tree for about 15 minutes until they refilled their tank and got it started again. Meanwhile, the guys couldn't stop laughing at me hiding behind the tree in the buff (with bugs and "skeeters" working on me) it was my turn to take the ribbing. I caught it for the rest of the evening. I was thankful there weren't many mosquitoes and "no-see-ums." We were all in bed before dark and again, had no "critter" visitors during the night.

### FIFTH DAY . . . Monday, April 21st
We broke camp early, and were on the water by **8:30 AM.** We arrived at the **Hwy. 75 bridge** at **11 AM.** Not long after we passed the 75 bridge, we discovered six or eight **_superb_** sandbar campsites.

If you love the outdoors and camping, **_this is the place._** This river has got to be one of the most beautiful and easiest paddles you'll ever experience. Don't miss this trip.

Just south of the **Hwy. 75** bridge, as we were moving silently down river, we surprised a 9 to 10' 'gator laying on the bank. He was the largest 'gator we saw *on the whole river trip.* As we swung around to get a picture of him, he plunged into the water like a pickup truck and we missed him. We eased back up stream the following morning by motor; but he was nowhere to be seen. I'm sure he heard the motor coming; where before we had been paddling *quietly* downstream. Several more times we had the same type huge fish come out of the water. We got a look at a couple of them but we were still baffled. We still had no idea what they were.

We had read about the river having great echoes, and decided to check it out. Sure enough! The echoes are exceptionally strong and clear. It's easy to see how the river got it's name *if* what we read about it being named "River of Echoes" in the Indian language; is true. We have heard at least five or six versions of how the river got its name. There are so many versions; one does not know which one to believe.

Someone had mentioned to us to "be sure and stop at **SUWANNEE SPRINGS**," so we stopped for about thirty minutes. It was interesting and we took pictures and video. It is easily recognized from the river. The first thing you will see is an extremely well built, wide, stairway of hewn stone going up into the park from the river (left side, right on a left bend). And a little farther down river, by the huge stone wall built 70 years ago around the spring to keep out river water. The spring was a famous resort in the 1920s. There isn't must left but the spring itself and the grounds are worth seeing. It was an interesting stop.

### END OF FIRST LEG OF TRIP
We arrived at the CANOE OUTPOST ramp, at the "SPIRIT OF THE SUWANNEE" Campground at **1:15 PM.** We had traveled **64 miles,** leisurely, in four and a half days. Roughly **23 hours of paddling time** . . . or about 3 MPH.

This <u>does not</u> take into consideration our 2 or 3 stretch stops, nor roughly 30 to 45 minutes for lunch each day. Also, we had been setting up camp at **3:30 to 4** every afternoon. That is quite *early.* You will probably wish to put down later in the day and get in more distance if you're on a tighter schedule. Remember, we were all retired! No time limits!

Back to the OUTPOST . . .

Van had brought his flatbed utility trailer on the trip and it came in *very* handy. Rather than load everything in our vans, he backed his trailer down to the water and we piled everything on it, leaving our canoes on the grass at the OUTPOST ramp.

At the campground office, we were told we could have our choice of any campsite we wanted in the tent area, so we opted for the ones closest to the showers. (The fee was **$12,** which included water and electric.) The electric was useful to recharge our camcorder and cellular phone batteries. (We brought a cellular phone along in case of an emergency.) I should also tell you that on the river, we found radios were of very little use. Though I did use the cell phone at Big Shoals to let our wives know all was well and it worked just fine. We hit those welcome hot showers early and they were heavenly. After we had showered and gotten into clean clothes, we inquired of one of the local workers as to who had **the best** and most reasonable food in town. We were told it was the **DIXIE GRILL** downtown on Hwy. 90, one block east of the 129 light. So we piled into Harry's van and headed for it.

It was an exceptionally good choice! The food was *superb* and the prices were reasonable. Randy is a seafood lover and ordered their "all you can eat" fresh mullet meal. He ate so much they ran out. They also have an excellent salad bar. We ate so much we were uncomfortable. We came out of the restaurant looking as if we all were going to "deliver twins" at any minute.

### SUPER STORE IN LAKE CITY

We each needed to resupply. Foods and also several camping items so again we piled into Harry's van and drove the 20 miles to Lake City's **WAL-MART.** It turned out to be a brand new **SUPER STORE.** We were astonished at the size. I believe it is one of the largest I have been in; and I have been in some big ones. They have *everything* under the sun. (Except they didn't have a replacement generator for my Coleman stove, so I had to buy a new stove.) We all needed grocery supplies and other items. We found their grocery section to be boundless. Including <u>block ice</u>, which is <u>not</u> available *anywhere else* in a 40 mile radius. We had checked on this before leaving. Block ice was the *main* reason for coming here to shop. Just in case you don't already know this (and you probably do), block ice will last twice as long as "cubed ice" . . . especially if you keep the cooler well protected from the sun. A solar blanket works wonders keeping out the heat. (See tips on this on page 75.)

For my "Boundry Waters" trip last year, I had purchased a new 4-man tent from **WAL-MART.** On the last day of this leg of the trip, somehow one of my tent poles cracked. (Luckily on the first leg and not the second.) So since we were going to WAL-MART in Lake City anyway, I took the broken pole with us.

*I didn't have my receipt, no record of purchase, only the damaged pole.* I showed the pole to the Manager of the Sporting Goods Dept., and gave him the model number of my tent and luck was with us. He had one on the shelf. I explained that we were on a long canoe trip and needed a replacement badly. I was extremely pleased when he broke open the new tent and gave me a replacement on the spot. <u>You can't beat service like that.</u> We resupplied our groceries, picked up several camping items, got block ice, our replacement pole, and were out of the store in about an hour. All of us were very pleased with the good service. They have so many checkout registers there is almost no wait to check out. We all agreed it was worth the 20-mile trip.

### SIXTH DAY . . . Tuesday, April 22
AT "SPIRIT OF THE SUWANNEE" CAMPGROUND
We slept later than usual this day since we had made the decision that we would stay an extra day here to resupply, wash clothes, reorganize and rest. We stored our fresh supplies, washed clothes and spent the rest of the day cleaning and reorganizing our gear. Randy and I decided to try our luck bass fishing in the little lake across the road from our site, but neither of us got a strike. This little lake, almost the size of a football field, looks like "bass heaven." It is lined with reeds and grasses, tall cypress trees and is a beautiful little natural lake. We had been told by the employees that there were some "big 'uns" in there. NOTE! On the evening of the *last day of our trip,* we again stayed here overnight to rest and get cleaned up for an early start home the following morning. (Remember, we had left our cars here.) As I came out of the shower, Randy called me over to another campsite. He said to me, "I want you to see this." An elderly gentleman opened up his large cooler and there was a beautiful *giant* bass. His *9-*

*year-old* grandson, *on his third cast,* (using a plastic worm) had hooked and landed this monster. My eyes popped out. WOW! NOW . . . we knew the employee was right. There are some monsters in that lake. The grandfather said the bass was over 8 pounds. We both felt a little sheepish since we hadn't even gotten a strike. However, we were happy for the nine-year-old for this bass will be a memory he will cherish the rest of his life.

Back to the trip . . . That evening, I made a last minute run into town to pick up a couple of items at **PUBLIX** Super Market (located on the far south edge of town on Hwy. 129). There is also a large **K-MART** there, and a laundromat. As I was leaving the store, I sniffed the air. There was a wonderful smell of barbecue in the air. I looked all around and suddenly there it was: **Ken's Bar-B-Que,** and in the same parking lot! I decided to treat the crew so I wheeled in and bought a couple lbs. of pork, a quart of barbecued beans, and some garlic bread to surprise them with a free meal. The food was superb but not having to cook was the best part. They cleaned it up in nothing flat as if they hadn't eaten in a week. After wonderful hot showers, we again turned in early for the big day ahead. Though we accomplished a lot here, we had a good rest.

### SEVENTH DAY . . . Wednesday, April 23rd

Since it would be faster and easier to eat out, we packed everything the night before. About 7:30 we all walked down to the restaurant inside the campground only to find it was not open. So we unhappily walked back to camp; again piling into Harry's van and went to the nearby **HUDDLE HOUSE** on 129 at I-10. It was good, fast and reasonable. Randy deliberately left his hat inside the van so he wouldn't leave it in the restaurant. When we got back to camp, we looked for it everywhere but it had disappeared. It was one of the mysteries of our trip. It was never found.

By the time we got our canoes and gear loaded, it was 10 AM. We left "SPIRIT OF THE SUWANNEE" about **10:15 AM.** About an hour later, we began to pass many beautiful sandbars. I should mention that on our first leg, we saw quite a few ducks, many hawks, an abundance of birds of all sorts (lots of cardinals), and farther downstream, an occasional osprey, and heard owls in the daylight. Though I have heard owls in the daytime before, it's not common.

By now, we had determined that every time we came across a beautiful sugar-sand sandbar, there almost always would be a **large** boil of water coming straight up near it. Not always was in in a bend. At first we thought it was springs coming in since the flow would be so great. Later, David Pharr of the OUTPOST told us he *thought* it was an upflow of water caused by hitting large limestone formations on the bottom. The more we thought about that, the more sense if made. Though there may be a *few* caused by large springs in the river bed, most probably are caused by deflected water. Whichever, it sure kicks a canoe off its direction in an instant.

We passed under **Hwy. 249** bridge at **3 PM.** We were told later there is drinking water available at **GIBSON PARK,** *at the ramp under the 249 bridge.* About 4 PM we began looking for the **SUWANNEE RIVER STATE PARK** Campground (#14 on the SRWMD "CANOE MAP"). But it was so poorly _marked on the river_, we missed it! We passed it by before we realized it. (As I began the editing of this edition, I called the Park Ranger and asked if they had installed a Park sign at the ramp yet. He told me they had not.) The only markings we saw from the river was a "WILDLIFE REFUGE" sign.

A little farther downstream from the sign was a concrete ramp. Since there was no identification at the ramp of any kind, we didn't think it was the Suwannee River State Park Campground, so we kept going. When we reached the Withlacoochee, we realized that the ramp must have been the camp-ground we were looking for but by then it was too late. There are **NO campsites** beyond that ramp to the WITHLACOOCHEE RIVER. We first checked out SUWANACOOCHEE SPRING, about 400 feet upstream on the left side of the WITHLACOOCHEE, but it didn't look too good. So we turned around and headed back to the Suwannee on the east side. *About 100 feet from the* SUWANNEE, we saw a spot that looked promising. We had to scramble up a high bank to determine if there was space there to camp. It turned out to be an excellent campsite. However, it had absolutely no markings of any kind seen from the river. We *later* discovered this nice site was the northern half of the **SUWANNEE RIVER STATE PARK.** It was **5:45 PM** when we pulled in there for the night.

Besides no markings, there was very little space to tie off the canoes (since the water was above normal). The embankment we had to crawl up with our gear was a steep gully. But once up on top, it was excellent. It is a well maintained, clean campsite; with picnic tables, fire ring, and room for 5 or 6 tents – maybe more!

Late in the afternoon, we again heard large fish jumping. They made such a loud splash; we guessed they were the same as we had seen upstream and were probably gar. After supper we sat around the fire for awhile discussing the day's events and as it got dark, one by one we headed for our sleeping bags.

### OWLS — "IN CONVERSATION!"

A couple of nights before, sitting around our campfire and listening to the owls close by, I told the fellows about the conversations owls hold when a bunch of them get together in one tree. Harry said, "I've never heard of such a thing." It had been dark about an hour or so and we were just getting comfortable in our bags when we got the treat of a lifetime. Harry got to hear the ***owls in conversation.*** There were at least four or five large owls in the trees **_directly above_** our tents. It really got noisy. **_Real Noisy!_** The chuckling, clucking, the hooting, hawing and the laughter that actually sounds like a raucous guffaw. It sounded like a bunch of old women telling dirty jokes.

One would start and the others would all chime in. As each one joined the laughing chorus, it sounded like he was trying to drown out the others. They would end that brief conversation with cackling that as I said, sounded exactly like a bunch of old women laughing. Then, it would start all over again. It was hilarious and lasted for about 30 minutes. It was one of those rare moments of our trip that I'm sure those guys will remember for a long time. Only twice before in my life had I heard owls like this, but they were not as near or as loud as this night.

This was a rare and wonderful treat. The next morning, I kicked myself for not recording it. Big mistake! I made a mental note that if we ever hear them again, if possible, I'll make *certain* I get it on tape. We also were close enough to the power plant to hear it humming all night but it was so faint it was not bothersome.

This campsite was eight hours by canoe from the **"SPIRIT OF THE SUWANNEE."** Roughly **19.5 miles** . . . our daily distance was improving. Don't forget the breaks.

### EIGHTH DAY . . . Thursday, April 24th

Again, we were up at the crack of daylight; ate and broke camp. It was a chore moving everything down the "gully" and loading. We pulled away at **8:15 AM.** Immediately after leaving the Withlacoochee, we had gone no more than a couple hundred yards when we spotted on the *right* bank, under the bridge (the **Seaboard Coast railroad** trestle and **Hwy. 90** are right together), what looked like a fair campsite. Easier canoe landing and launching on a small sandy beach but it lacked any of the amenities of the other campsite.

Only minutes below the bridge, we passed what looked like a large canal on the right. I believe this is from **ELLAVILLE SPRING.** We hadn't gone far when again, another huge fish jumped out of the water and made a splash like he had dropped from the sky. We still didn't know what the darn things were. A little farther on, there was another big one.

A short distance down river, on the left, we saw the two canals from the SUWANNEE RIVER FPL POWER PLANT. Just below that, we came to small rapids that were quite turbulent; however, they were *nothing* compared to BIG SHOALS. We ran them with little effort. In fact, it was an exhilarating short ride (at high water). On this stretch we found very few places to pull out, much less camp. A short time later we passed two fellows fishing from a boat and asked what the huge jumping fish were that we had been seeing for the last few days. We were very surprised to hear they were **STURGEON!** They said they come into the Suwannee to spawn in the spring, then one never sees or hears them the rest of the year.

### BEAUTIFUL SMALL SPRING!

Approximately between ¼ and ½ mile below the power plant on the right, we came upon a beautiful, crystal clear, tiny spring boiling up *right at the edge of the river.* It probably was no wider than 2-3 feet. Until this point, every spring we had seen was flowing water almost as dark as the main river. (Probably due to mixing at high water.) It was crystal clear and clean and bubbling up from a small hole, less than a foot from the edge of the river, making it extremely easy to make use of. In my opinion, this spring would be an excellent place to refill all of ones drinking water containers. Obviously, the water level would be the main factor. If the water is too high, you might never see it. I asked SRWD if it had a name and I was told it did not.

Though I *personally* would have no qualms about drinking this water, to be on the safe side, it would be best to consult those who know more about this than I. As in somebody from the Suwannee River Water Management office! I'm sure *you* would not, however, for the record, I definitely would **NOT** recommend drinking Suwannee River water without first boiling it for at least five minutes.

About noon, we found a beautiful sandbar at a right bend of the river. We stopped for a long lunch and a good stretch. We found this bar to be an excellent campsite that would hold a dozen canoes as well as five or six tents. (Judging by time, my guess is that it was about 10 miles below the WITHLACOOCHEE.) Again, there were more sturgeon, and they appeared larger.

On the left side, about one and a half miles before **DOWLING PARK,** is a small campsite that will handle 3 or 4 tents. Then about one half mile farther on, in the left bend in the river, there is a beautiful huge sandbar. It looks as if it gets plenty of use. This was one of the largest and prettiest sandbars we had seen on the river until now. Since it was nearing 3 PM, we thought we would put down here and started paddling toward it only to find upon closer observation, it was occupied. About one half mile farther on, on the left side, we discovered a nice concrete ramp, a couple of canoes on the bank; and a very large grassy area with picnic tables. It was obvious this was private property, so the crew waited at the ramp while Randy and I went downstream by motor, checking for another site. As we rounded a right bend, we determined this was **DOWLING PARK.**

There was a large sign posted high on a very large modern decking with steps coming all the way down to the river; with a floating dock to tie up. We continued downstream for a short distance, found nothing, so we decided to come back and ask permission to camp on the grassy site. We docked at the floating dock and went up to the main buildings.

The beautiful **VILLAGE LODGE** is located here. Asking directions, we found the property manager at the Lodge office. We explained who we were and our situation, guaranteeing her that if permitted to camp there overnight, we would leave no trace of our having been there. Her name was **DOT,** and she was very cordial, checked our ID and graciously granted us permission. We discovered that we were on a 1,000-acre *retirement village*, owned and operated by the **SEVENTH-DAY ADVENTISTS** church.

As we left the office, we noticed they also had a small but nice grocery store there. We went in and grabbed a few supplies and were off to join the others in a flash. We were all tired after having bucked head winds most of the afternoon and didn't wish to travel much farther. So they were pleased when they heard we had permission to camp there. And even more pleased we had brought ice.

We set up camp on the well-cut grass alongside a large pavilion which the church group had used for cookouts (though it looked like it had not been used in years). However, it suited our needs nicely and we made good use of it. The pavilion has a very large roof and is open on all sides. We camped beside the building on the green grass.

***However,*** I DON'T ADVISE USING THIS SITE WITHOUT FIRST GETTING PERMISSION. *THEY HAVE ARMED ROVING SECURITY GUARDS.* IF YOU ARE NOT PREAUTHORIZED, THEY'LL MAKE YOU LEAVE.

Though the grocery store was small, we found it to be extremely well equipped. For those who need to **_RE-SUPPLY,_** this would do fine. They *do* have ice, but it's crushed only. For those using an outboard, with so many cars, there must be a gas station nearby. We estimated we had traveled **16.8** miles today.

### NINTH DAY . . . April 24th

We left DOWLING PARK at **8 AM,** made a second quick stop at the store for miscellaneous items for everybody and moved on downstream. The wind suddenly came up and was extremely strong and it was laborious paddling since we were struggling right into it. We decided to put in early again and get a fresh start in the morning so we stopped for the day at **LAFAYETTE BLUE SPRINGS, at 3 PM.** It is on the right and can be recognized by a large cove back off the river with a set of nicely built wooden stairs coming down to the water.

View looking from the back toward the river. There is a natural bridge between the wooden stairs, about 10' wide, open underneath and very deep water on each side.

It is a very large spring with a natural limestone bridge across the center. The spring is clear with a very high volume flow. They also have shower facilities and tent camping. The canoe pull-out has a good sandy beach with the tent sites on the flat about ten feet above the river and at the river's edge. The sites have fresh water. They have cold drinks, etc., at the small stand at the front gate of the park but not much else. They have no ice or supplies. But they do have plenty of hot water in the showers. You must register to camp, and the fee is **$10 per site.** Be sure to see the other large spring that is there also, a 100 yards or so inland from the main spring. During the evening we heard several more sturgeon.

### TENTH DAY, SATURDAY . . . April 25th
We left **LAFAYETTE BLUE SPRINGS** at **8 AM.** There seemed to be a noticeable increase in the speed of the river here; at least that was our impression. At about **10 AM,** we passed under the **HWY. 51** bridge. *About 30 minutes later* we rounded a right bend and suddenly there was a piece of Florida history. The open draw bridge, still standing in the middle of the river is part of the second RR ever built in Florida. A silent sentry of the past, it was impressive and an almost mystical sight.

The "Drew" drawbridge, a piece of Florida's history. Rounding a right bend, suddenly there it is, standing like a sentinel of the past. We stopped for several minutes to admire it.

Again more *"flying sturgeon."* A couple came up close to us and about an hour later one came up right between the canoes of Van and Harry and scared them out of their wits. They jokingly said that they needed to pull out at the next sandbar and clean themselves. We all died laughing. Later we saw some local fishermen and asked what we should use for bait for sturgeon. We were told that it is illegal and a heavy fine to bother them in any way so we quickly put *that* idea to rest.

Coming down river, we again tried out the echoes and they were exceptional. We amused ourselves testing them for several minutes, when Van popped up and accused us of acting like little kids. We all busted out laughing. Laughing, Harry said, *"we don't care . . . we're having fun!"* (Harry was 73 years old then.) About **3 PM** we estimated we had traveled roughly **20 miles.** The weekend recreational boats and "jet skis" had suddenly become very heavy. (This was Saturday.) Since we had been putting down about this time anyway, we looked for and found a nice campsite on the right, where there is an old *"closed"* dirt ramp about *2 miles north* of **TROY SPRINGS.** It was a nice campsite up high, on flat and level ground, with a good place to beach the canoes.

We stop for a stretch break and enjoy the cool shade on one of the beautiful sandbars. There are **many** of these from Hwy. 75 to Dowling Park. However, *very few* after.

Apparently, the state had stopped people from putting boats in there by blocking off the dirt ramp with large posts in the ground. That is what you should look for. They are easily seen if you are running near the right bank. It was also a dead-end road turnaround and appeared to be well used. Throughout the day we had several pickups and a couple of cars show up; though all quickly turned around and left. (They were mostly young kids so when they saw us old goats; they hi-tailed it out of there fast.)

That afternoon, since we were so close, I decided to go into **BRANFORD**. I put the motor in and headed downstream to town. I wanted to make sure we still had permission from the DIVE SHOP owner, **Gene Broome,** to camp on his property (it had been over a month since I had gotten his permission). I also wanted to pick up a couple of things at the store. I was roughly 8 miles to town. That was a long way with a 3 HP motor. Going downstream, it took an hour and fifteen minutes. I calculated it would take me more than double that time returning against the current. My calculations were right on target! It took me two and a half hours exactly to get back to camp *against* the current.

It was just getting dark as I pulled into camp. The crew was already getting uneasy and were preparing to put lights at the canoes if I had been much later. They were glad to see me, *especially since I had brought back ice, ice cold "beverages" and a newspaper.* We had been without news of the outside world for several days. The ice cold "beverage" was a treat at the end of a long day.

Since it was Saturday and there were so many power boats and jet skis, we decided it would be better to wait out the weekend where we were rather than have to put up with constant wakes from the pleasure boaters. Sunday being even worse since it was the busiest day on the river. We had *been warned* by two different people **not** to be on the lower river *on the weekend, especially* the area between **BRANFORD** and the **SANTA FE RIVER** junction. Also, it looked and felt like rain, so we made our decision to stay put and settled in, put tarps over everything and prepared for it, though it never came.

Late that evening, a large horned owl lit in the tree right above the campsite and began his song. He got in several good calls before Randy grabbed up the camcorder and began to record him. The commotion on the ground unsettled him so he got out of there fast. Randy did get a good shot of him and his calls on video. We heard lots of owls again this night. They were all over the place. But no "conversations" like we had heard at SUWANNEE RIVER STATE PARK.

We had seen a lot of animal tracks all along the river's edge when we pulled in so we were sure we would get "critters" during this night . . . but we didn't. Again we attributed our good fortune to Van who scared them away with his snoring. We jokingly told him it sounded like a pack of wild hogs on the rampage and no respectable 'coon in his right mind would dare come into camp. We all had a good laugh and he laughed along with us, taking the ribbing goodnaturedly.

### ELEVENTH DAY . . . SUNDAY, April 26th
We enjoyed the leisure of taking it easy all day Sunday. The river traffic was extremely heavy with large pleasure craft and many jet skis passing constantly. We commented that we sure were glad we had laid over! We rested mostly, using some of the time to reorganize, cleaned our equipment and canoes, and did a little fishing.

## TWELFTH DAY . . . MONDAY, April 27th

We had gotten everything ready for an early morning launch the night before, so we ate, packed up and were on the river by **7:30 AM.** One of the reasons for leaving early, was the group had decided to stop only briefly for supplies in **BRANFORD.** (The original plan had been to lay over there and re-supply.) They reasoned that since it was only 8 miles, and would be so early when we arrived, they didn't want to waste the half day, since they had lounged an extra day already. They theorized they would rather use the rest of the afternoon to get farther down river. All agreed, so that's what we did.

On our way to BRANFORD, we stopped a few minutes to take a look at **TROY SPRINGS.** We were told TROY has no camping, though it is pretty and lots of picnickers and boaters go there. Access is off the right side of the river, and they have a small dock and a ramp. Down river on the left about a mile or so, is **LITTLE RIVER SPRINGS.** They had a stairway, and when I had passed Saturday evening, there were at least a hundred teens and college kids all along the banks so it must be very popular in the summer.

## BRANFORD . . . END OF SECOND LEG!

Arriving in town at **10:30,** we quickly gathered supplies, made phone calls to our families, and were on our way by **11:30.** Branford is a good place to **re-supply.** From where you pull out (or tie up), the store is only about 100 yards from the river; right at the edge of the parking lot. Though it is a convenience store, they have most of the things you might need. I should mention that BRANFORD has an "inside spring" of its own in a nice little cove-like area, accessible from the river about a hundred feet north of the concrete ramp. It is ringed with cedar decking and a dock where one may tie up. It is on the left a couple hundred yards past the bridge. Above the public concrete ramp and to the right is a picnic park. The park is set up with about four picnic tables, and Ramada's. Signs state *"NO overnight camping allowed"* in this park.

If your group is not large, in a pinch one could probably get permission from **Gene Broome,** the owner of the **"BRANFORD DIVE CENTER"** (located over the ramp) by asking permission in advance. His area is only large enough for four or five *small* tents, and is the grassy area immediately north of the ramp. It is also *private property!* PLEASE . . . DO NOT CAMP HERE

WITHOUT ASKING! If he is nice enough to allow you to use it
. . . (and he probably will) <u>please</u> . . . make certain it's cleaner
than it was when you arrived. Abuse it and river travelers might
not be allowed to use it again! <u>You</u> might need it again some day!

We had been warned that there were **no campsites for
quite a long distance below BRANFORD,** and they were
right. *We did not see a single campsite that was usable all the
way to within one third of a mile of the **SANTA FE RIVER.*** On
the left side, about one third of a mile before the junction, there
is a huge, *beautiful,* sugar-sand sandbar. As previously mentioned, we were also relying on Clyde Council's "SUWANNEE
COUNTRY" guide and therefore we passed up this wonderful
spot looking for the site on the south bank of the SANTA FE,
he pointed to in his guide.

Though he was correct in that there were no campsites
down to this point of the river, the description and location of
the campsite at the junction with the SANTA FE RIVER was
incorrect. COUNCIL'S guide indicated the site was at the south
corner, on the point at the SANTA FE. All of this land is WELL
POSTED, as well as all of the land on the north side. There was
**only one** site close to this location. It was on the SUWANNEE
a hundred feet **past** the junction, on the **right – not on the
left.** It was a nice site; but narrow; and not near as nice as the
sandbar we had passed a third of a mile back. The swift
current at this point and our being too tired to work against it,
we made the decision not to go back to the beautiful sandbar.
This one was *much smaller,* but it had a good sandy beach for
the canoes, and though it had limited tent space; we put down
here (see picture on next page). If you need more space and opt
for this little beach, if necessary, there is another flat area
about 40 feet inside the woods where more tents could be set
up. The main thing I liked about this site was that it was
'almost' directly across from the SANTA FE river mouth. Since
I wanted to fish in the SANTA FE, it was handy to just pop
across the river and right into the mouth of the other. There
were a few mosquitoes on the beach here; but not bad.
However, inside the wooded area was a different story. They
were hungry, lots of them, and a nuisance.

Randy and I set up early intending to sleep out under the stars. We quickly abandoned that idea when we heard thunder close by. It wasn't long after that a monster storm hit us.

## CHECKING OUT "BASS COUNTRY!"

That afternoon was so pleasant that we decided not to put up our tent. We set up camp to sleep out under the stars.

It was still early in the afternoon so Randy and I decided to go across the check out the bass possibilities at the mouth of the SANTA FE. We had gone only a short distance, when we came to what looked like an opening in the cypress trees on the left. We eased our canoe between the trees and there was a *beautiful* 'backwater' area with about two or three feet of water. This looked like **"BASS COUNTRY"** for certain so we paddled slowly in and began casting plastic worms. In no time I had hooked three bass and boated one.

Randy also hooked three but lost them all. He returned to camp disheartened but cheered up and happily cleaned my fish when I told him I didn't eat much fish anyway. (He loves fish!) We told the others about this beautiful area so we took our cameras and went back for pictures. We tried fishing again late in the day just before dark, but to no avail. They quit biting as if someone had slammed the door. It wasn't long before we learned why.

## STORM!

Late that evening, we had finished supper and were sitting around the fire enjoying the beautiful displays of what we thought was distant "heat lightning" dancing over the southwestern sky. We began to notice it seemed to be getting closer. When we began to hear distinctive rumbling of thunder, we said **"UH OH!"** and began scrambling to get our tent up (in the dark) and make preparations for rain. We quickly threw up our tent and began to lash everything down, including the canoes. They still had some equipment in them and in my haste, I made a <u>bad decision</u> to cover them. I knew proper procedure was to cover the unused equipment *with the canoe* upside down over it. I had done it many times, but in my haste to get ready for this storm that was bearing down on us fast, I made a ***bad decision.***

We had no sooner started back from the canoes when the *monsoon* hit. It started raining as if someone had turned the river upside down on us . . . Van, who normally slept out, quickly joined us in our tent since we had plenty of room. *OOPS!* We quickly discovered we had <u>two</u> leaks . . . and ***both*** *of them* were in the area where poor ole Van was laying. We were on a slightly slanted surface so a tiny bit of water came in at the bottom edge and ran down to him; then we got another leak, right at top center, directly above him. The wind was fierce and kept changing direction; so we were hit with driving rain first on one side, then the other.

Van was uncomfortable under the leaks but not as much as he would have been had he remained outside. There was the usual amount of humorous banter and scurrying about trying to keep things dry, but we managed well otherwise. Niagara Falls poured *all night.* Next morning, it was still raining. Van ribbed us for days about our leaky tent.

Since Randy and I had waterproofed everything <u>*extremely well*</u> just before leaving on the trip, we couldn't imagine what caused the tent to leak. Granted it was a deluge, but we had been well prepared for it. On close examination the next morning, I discovered that in our haste, and in the dark, somehow we had mistakenly laid the top *rainfly,* "single pole support," laying across <u>the tent material,</u> rather than above and across the top of the main cross poles where it was supposed to be. That put the pole in direct contact with the material on top of the tent, therefore creating an osmosis effect. We learned our lesson. Never again!

However, we didn't easily find the cause of the dribbling leak at the floor bottom. Upon closer inspection later under a magnifying glass, I discovered the needle the manufacturer had used to sew, apparently was a big one so the holes were much too large for the thread used. The factory apologized and sent me three bottles of free seam-sealer. I resealed all the seams around where the floor joined the walls, *inside and out* and they have never leaked since. I mention this boring event only to alert you so that hopefully you can prevent these "goofs" and have a safer and more enjoyable trip. *(With No leaks!)*

### THIRTEENTH DAY . . . Tuesday, April 28th
### Bad Decision!

When we awoke early the next morning, it was still raining. I could hear Harry, Van and Ray scurrying around outside trying to make coffee in the rain; I chuckled to myself and rolled over and went back to sleep. Randy did the same. Along about **9 AM** the rain eased up and we crawled out bleary eyed and found some breakfast. Shortly, I wandered down to the canoe to check it out, then let out a screeching yell. It was **FULL** of water. I had expected <u>some</u> water . . . but not *THAT* much! There must have been 200 gallons in it. It was almost to the top of the gunwales even though we had covered <u>most</u> of the canoe with a large tarp. Being far too heavy to tilt, we had to bail and everything we had left in it was a mess. Fortunately, there was nothing in it that could be *damaged* by water. Though I had made a lattice floor specifically to keep our supplies up off the bottom in case of rain, there was so much rain, it was useless. Water was into everything. Next time, we'll unload and turn the canoe over as we should have done in the first place. *BAD DECISION!* The weather began to clear about 10 AM, so we decided to stay put another day to try to dry everything out. It was a strange sight. There were clotheslines everywhere.

Later that afternoon I decided to go back and enjoy more of that wonderful *"Bass Country"* across the river. Randy declined since he was tired so I went by myself. I had been inside that "unreal bass heaven" no more than 20 minutes and had already *again* hooked 3 but landed only one.

Right after I landed my bass, once again; as suddenly as if someone slammed the gate, they stopped biting. I fished for 2 more hours, moving slowly, casting around all logs, cypress trees and stumps and never got another strike. Randy was pleased that he now had a second bass for his supper that night. I estimated this one was about two and a half to three pounds. Slightly larger than the one I caught the day before.

Paddling back to camp I chuckled as I looked at our campsite, it looked like "wash day in the country." There were clotheslines everywhere. Van's clothes had been in heavy brown garbage bags in his canoe, so he felt comfortable they were safe from the weather. WRONG! His bags had not been _doublebagged_. Somewhere along the way they had gotten punctured; so when the canoe filled with water, so did his clothes bags. Everything he had was soaked. Harry got a good fire going under one of the clotheslines to help dry things. Nothing more was said about it on the trip, however, _at our reunion cookout at Harry's place after the trip,_ Ray piped up and said, "I never want to dry my clothes over a fire again!" We all looked at him quizzically and asked . . . "why?" He said with a sheepish grin, _"after two weeks I still can't get rid of the smell of smoke in my underwear."_ Everybody busted out laughing, including all of our wives.

### FOURTEENTH DAY . . . Wednesday, April 29th
### – RE-SUPPLY POINT –
(and another boo-boo!)

Again up early, we were on the river by **8 AM.** About an hour and a half down river, I noticed our fishing rods were not where they had usually been packed so I asked Randy where he had packed them. He turned to me and said, **_"Oh my gosh!_** I don't remember packing them; they must be still leaning against the tree on the beach." I hadn't packed them either, so it became obvious we had left them . . . at least five miles back **and** against the current.

_It was here that I was very thankful_ I had the little Johnson outboard. Had we not had it, some very expensive rod and reels would have been gone forever. I would not have paddled back five miles against _that_ current for them.

We shouted our dilemma to the others and told them to go on ahead, we'd catch up later. I fired up the motor and headed back upstream. It seemed like ages before we rounded the bend and had the beach in sight. _UH OH!_ There, less than a hundred feet or so just past where the rods had been left standing, were two fellows moving slowly downstream fishing, _very_ close to the bank. They obviously had just passed the rods only minutes before. I just _knew_ they had picked up our rods. But we got lucky; when we pulled up to the beach there they were, leaning against the tree roots on the beach right where Randy had left them. What a close call – and a boo boo. Thank heaven I had brought the 3 horse.

Though we were returning downstream by motor, it seemed like we would never catch up. It seemed like hours before we spotted the others under the **Hwy. 340** bridge at **ROCK BLUFF.** It turned out that they had just pulled in to wait for us only minutes before. By now it was **11 AM.**

It worked out well since we had to stop there anyway for supplies. **At** the *340 bridge at ROCK BLUFF,* there is a **General Store and gas station** at the edge of the parking lot; adjacent to the ramp. It has just about anything you might need.

We had just returned from the grocery and sat down on the small retaining wall next to the ramp to eat lunch when we heard a shout, *"you guys come on up here and use my picnic table."* We looked up to see a friendly grinning face. He lived above and right next to the ramp. We happily joined him and made good use of his table. It was a huge concrete picnic table with a stainless steel top. That was a pleasant surprise. After the usual introductions we sat down to eat. A few minutes later we got another nice surprise when he brought out fresh garden onions to go with our meal and sat down with us. His name was *Art Hagen,* and he lived in ST. PETERSBURG (we later discovered). He graciously offered us the use of his outside toilet facilities (which were modern flush) and even a shower if we wished.

We all sat at his nice picnic table; eating and swapping stories. It was a very nice chance meeting with this man. It is rare in this day and time when a man will offer total strangers the hospitality as he did. As we were finishing our lunch, he went back into the house and brought each of us a large golden delicious apple. Everybody commented on how sweet and juicy they were. We said our "good-byes" and headed back for the river. It was agreed this guy was an exceptional and truly rare person.

I almost forgot to mention, that <u>we **did not** see one</u> possible *campsite, all the way from the **SANTA FE RIVER to the 340 Bridge.** But . . . <u>LOTS</u> of houses!* North of the SANTA FE we saw <u>very few</u> houses. South of the SANTA FE, they are thick on both sides; all the way to 340.

After stowing our fresh supplies, we got underway again about **12:30** then went back upstream a little less than a quarter mile to see **ROCK BLUFF SPRINGS.** Art had mentioned that we should not miss seeing them. They are set back in, about 300 yards through a narrow winding opening. Going into the spring we saw hundreds of fresh water mullet, a few nice bass, turtles and other fish. The spring was quite pretty and worth going back for. Inside, the main spring is very deep and flows crystal clear. Many people come here to swim. However, the grounds are private and POSTED. It is quite large and there are two very large cypress trees growing about 20 feet from the concrete wall. Though since the water was high; these trees may normally have been at the edge of a little beach which we could not see. It was an interesting stop.

A mile or so *below* Hwy. 340, we passed **GUARANTO SPRINGS Campground** on the right. It appears to have good camping and landing sites. We didn't stop so we don't know how large it is; however, from the water, it looked nice and quite large. They also have a good ramp.

Approximately *four miles* below the 340 bridge, we came to **WANNEE** (Village of), a huge campground on the left that looked as if it could support twenty canoes and thirty tents with ease. It was nice and flat with large oak trees and lots of green grass, about 10 feet above the river and had a great beach and ramp. On this day it was empty. However, I'm sure this place is jumping on the weekends. It sure was pretty. We stopped just long enough to stretch, and check it out for future use.

Three or four miles farther on, *on the left*, we came to **SUN SPRINGS** and settlement. It was very pretty with lots of nice little houses on a canal. We were looking for a place to pull out and eat supper when a resident there told us there were none in that area; but she said there <u>was</u> a place a half mile farther down, on the left. A few minutes later we found it, and it was a nice one. It was called **EULA LANDING.** There is also a *large* lodge there, called **EULA LODGE.** The picnic grounds are spacious and there are many large oak trees. However, there are *not many picnic tables.* There was a County sign posted there, stating ***"NO OVERNIGHT CAMPING ANYWHERE ON THE RIVER IN THIS COUNTY EXCEPT AT HART SPRINGS CAMPGROUND!"*** (This was Gilchrist County.) Also, we *did not see ANYTHING* that looked like a usable campsite, other than at the Hart Springs Campground . . . and all the way to just north of OLDTOWN, *and that was a* **K.O.A.** about two miles north of OLDTOWN. (Phone Number in back.)

### MOONLIGHT CANOEING!
It was at the EULA LANDING picnic area, that the group hatched the idea to canoe by moonlight; since there was a full

moon that night. They had read of canoeing by moonlight in another book and decided to try it; it would be a great experience. We all agreed, and after supper we hit the river again. This would turn out to be our longest day on the river. We traveled a little over **30 MILES** on this day. Late in the day we passed **HART SPRINGS** on the left but didn't stop. However, the campground looked large, had a nice ramp and plenty of good sandy beach for canoes. We could also see quite a few cement picnic tables.

The moon came up early and as the sun slowly settled, we marveled at the beauty of the river at sundown. After it had gone down, we found that we had plenty of light. We could see for a mile or more. The moon was full, the water was like glass, the sky was crystal clear and the smell of the forest was sweet and clean. Not a sound could be heard except for the dipping of paddles, tree frogs singing and owls calling from deep in the forest. As we glided silently down the middle of the river, *it was a superb outdoor experience we will never forget!* Ray summed up all of our feelings when he said: ***"Umm umm! It don't get any better than this!"*** He was right! All down river for the last 10 days, the jokes, the banter, the chatter, had been incessant. For the first time on the whole trip the group fell very silent, savoring the sweetness of the moment.

*Then the silence was suddenly shattered!* During the day we had seen at least a dozen sturgeon jumping, now in the dark; occasionally we would hear a loud splash. Suddenly one jumped less than 10 feet from Van's canoe. After the surprise had worn off, Van joked about hoping those 100-lb. sturgeons were able to see in the dark. He didn't want one of them joining him in his canoe. We all had another good laugh!

I have to say I believe this night to be one of the major highlights of the trip. *It was indescribably wonderful!* Believe it or not, we had zero mosquitoes this night.

### OLDTOWN and a MOTEL!

About **10:30 PM,** we were tired from the long day. Our bottoms felt as if they had turned to concrete as we began looking for a campsite. We could see the KOA lights at the river's edge from a *very long distance;* though from a distance, we had no idea what they were. It was extremely well lit. As we got closer, we saw what it was and made the mistake of passing it by. We were hoping to find a non-commercial place to camp.

That was a mistake! We continued on without finding anything until we saw a large grassy area with a huge long dock. We decided to ask for permission to camp there. By now it was after **11 PM**. It turned out to be **SUWANNEE GABLES MOTEL AND MARINA.**

The owner apologetically told us that according to the law, she could not allow us to camp on the property or she could lose her license. We decided we were too tired to continue down river looking in the dark; so all agreed to pull up here at the motel rather than risk not being able to find anything so late. So by **11:30** we had checked in. The lady was pleasant and did give us a special rate.

The **Suwannee Gables Motel** has a super large and modern dock big enough to tie up 15 or 20 canoes at one time. Clean and reasonable with a great restaurant across the street.

Her dock appeared to be well over 150 feet long and was almost new so we had a great place with plenty of room to safely secure our canoes. The best part was that we didn't have to unload anything but clean clothing and toilet articles. The rooms were nice, clean, modern and roomy. Best of all, *there was plenty of that wonderful **hot water**.* After showering for what seemed like hours, we all passed out in sweet bliss!

**FIFTEENTH DAY . . . Thursday, April 30th**

Again up early, we headed for the restaurant *across the street*. Bacon, eggs, biscuits and hot coffee sounded wonderful. As we were walking toward the street, Van wise cracked about being stiff in the back from "sleeping on a darn bed." (There was nothing wrong with the beds.) After him sleeping on the hard ground most of the trip, we cracked up with laughter. Just as we were starting to cross the street, we were stopped by two senior couples from **VERO BEACH** who were attempting to travel all of Florida's major waterways, *by PONTOON BOAT*. They had just arrived the night before and were heading home. They asked a lot of questions about our trip and were very nice people. After we arrived at the restaurant, we spoke with some Wildlife Officers who were eating breakfast.

We questioned them about camping facilities farther down river. They said, *"there are **none** all the way from **FANNIN SPRINGS to YELLOW JACKET,** and YELLOW JACKET was the **last campground** before the gulf."* At the time we thought that bad news but it turned out to be no problem since we didn't need a campsite other than Yellow Jacket anyway.

However, they were correct, <u>there were none all the way to the Gulf</u>. I should tell you also that I recently spoke with the owner of the little Grocery store at FOWLERS BLUFF. He told me that several times canoers had been caught in bad weather and he had allowed them to camp there. You might keep that in mind if you are going to make the trip. However, if possible, you should stop at YELLOW JACKET since they have full camping facilities. Fowler's Bluff has no camping facilities, though they *do* have cabins.

Back to the restaurant . . . After finishing a *wonderful* breakfast, we quickly gathered our things and headed for the docks. We were surprised to see the owner of the Motel had come out to see our canoes and see us off. She was a very nice lady with a great personality. The two couples traveling by pontoon boat also were there to see us off and wished us a safe trip. We were pleasantly surprised at the sudden attention we were receiving. We left the docks about **8:10 AM,** and headed down river.

Just as we rounded the bend, less than a quarter mile on the right side and under the Hwy. 19-98 bridge, @#$%*!^* there was a small sandy area that we probably could have used to put down, *had we only known.* But we were satisfied under the circumstances; it had worked out well. It is not a campsite, but one could get by there in a pinch. Probably without getting in trouble with the county since it is *right on the county line.* It might be worth keeping in mind, just in case.

After going under the bridge, we had gone only a very short distance when we arrived at **FANNIN SPRINGS** *on the left.* We paddled 100 feet or so in to see them and they were very pretty. We were there about 15 minutes; then headed down river. Along the left bank, we saw 5 or 6 ***very*** *small* sandy beaches one might stop on in a pinch.

The LEVY County line starts at FANNIN SPRINGS, so you are in a different county than you were at HART SPRINGS. We didn't see any signs regarding LEVY County laws on river camping; there are a few very small sandy sites here. <u>Very few and very small!</u>

### MANATEE SPRINGS

About noon, as we were approaching the entrance into MANATEE SPRINGS, we saw three deer at river's edge. There is a steel cable across the entrance to the spring, with a sign saying **"CANOES ONLY — NO MOTORIZED BOATS."** The cable was low enough in the water that we were able to pass over it with no problem.

Manatee Springs has a super picnic grounds, lots of picnic tables, clean restrooms, and the spring is cold, clear and beautiful. **Great** place to take the family.

For those traveling by power boat, there is a nice dock and ramp located just past the entrance. It has a fine wooden walkway all the way up to the spring. When we arrived at the spring, we were surprised to find the group of young boys from the Sheriff's Boys Ranch that we had seen late that evening when we were camped at BIG SHOALS. It seems that somewhere they had gotten ahead of us. MANATEE SPRINGS was their final destination. They were swimming, running, yelling and having a blast. The group had made themselves a special flag from an old sheet and called themselves "The lost boys."

We spoke with them at great length, and noted a definite change in attitude and manners of the kids at the end of their trip; from what we had seen at the SHOALS. It was remarkable. We agreed it was much better. They had just completed a 180-mile canoe trip and it was obvious they were proud of their accomplishment. They had every right to be and I'm sure it is something they will remember the rest of their lives.

MANATEE SPRINGS is one of the prettiest and largest of the springs and the nicest campground we saw on the whole trip, not to mention that the flow is unbelievable. The cold water is crystal clear and flows **116 MILLION gallons a day.** The campground was very large with lots of picnic tables, clean restrooms, canoe ramp, phones, great swimming facilities, and a snack bar.

After having lunch at their snack shop, taking lots of pictures and doing a quick recon of the place, at **2:00 PM** we left the springs and continued down river. At this point, the river becomes **very** wide. About a mile later, we saw our first large patch of lily pads on the river. Since there were many and extended quite a ways into the river, I decided to video tape them. We began paddling slowly directly through them. Randy was up front filming. We had gone about 50 feet into the pads when we came to a small open space of water (5 or 6 ft. in dia.). As we were easing through it we heard a splash and a loud thump on the bottom of the canoe.

We had apparently surprised a large bass (or a small 'gator) snoozing. He hit the bottom of the canoe with a thump as he cleared out of there. Though we were filming at the time, we didn't get the UFO on film but we sure got the loud thump when he banged his "whatever" against our canoe. Whatever it was, neither of us saw it. About noon, *there was no place to pull out*

From Hwy. 340 on, the river continues to widen. From Manatee Springs on, it really gets wide. This is about a mile or so past Manatee Springs, Note the lily pads.

*for lunch* so we ate lunch tied up to a large log sticking up out of the water about 50 feet out from the river bank. While eating, Van said, "look over there," pointing to the shore. There was a fair size 'gator laying in the weeds watching us.

Yellow Jacket is on the right. Look for the boats and houseboats. The small sign is hard to read from a distance but you will have no trouble identifying the campground.

## YELLOW JACKET!

We pulled in at YELLOW JACKET Campground a little after **3 PM.** This campground is *"almost"* halfway from **FANNIN SPRINGS** (13 miles) to the town of **SUWANNEE** (32 total). It can be recognized by a large brown building on stilts, lots of houseboats and a small sign on a tree above the sandy ramp. The owner, Rich, told me they have 100 RV sites and 25 tent sites, several large tent sites alongside the river. They have picnic tables, running water, and electric. But at our site beside the river, the electric had not been completed, only the wires were there. They had good hot showers. The charge was **$10 a site** with a $2 charge per extra person. They also have a small dock at the tent site area you can use to tie up as well as the sandy ramp.

Rich is a retired police officer and lives here with his own *"menagerie."* He had horses, chickens, bantam roosters by the dozen, ducks (more than 50), 6 or 7 dogs, a tom turkey that must have been more than 10 years old, peacocks, geese, parrots . . . you name it he had it. AND . . . he had his *own private stock* of "NO-SEE-UMS" by the zillions. Old tom turkey decided he wanted to get chummy with us and kept strutting into our site while we were setting up. He was a stubborn cuss. We almost had to shove him to get him to leave. After a half dozen tries, each time getting shooed away, he finally got the message and slowly ambled off disgusted with our hospitality.

As one can imagine, it was a little noisy here but it was a pleasurable and interesting stop. *And* . . . it was the *ONLY* one available. The Rangers were right! We *did not see anything* that even looked like it could be used to camp on, all the way from FANNIN SPRINGS to the town of SUWANNEE, **except YELLOW JACKET,** and MAYBE . . . FOWLER'S BLUFF in an emergency (discussed earlier).

Back to YELLOW JACKET . . . Along about evening I decided to take my canoe and try the lily pads hoping for a big bass. Randy declined so I left him on the dock trying for catfish. I did hook a couple (on plastic worms) but lost them both. As the sun went down I was still working the pads. And the **no-see-ums** were working on me. (I had forgotten to bring my repellent with me.)

As the sun dropped, I switched to a "Jitterbug" and began working the outer edges of the lily pads. I had made six or eight casts when suddenly I noticed a wake coming after it. I thought "Here comes a big one," I first thought it was a large bass but there was something strange about this wake . . . it was too slow . . . Suddenly, I realized it was not a fish at all . . . it was a baby 'gator about 4 feet, and he wanted that lure badly. I pulled it away from him several times only to have him try for it again on the next cast!

It was fun, yet I knew better than to let him catch it. After awhile he gave up; reluctantly, so did I since it was getting dark and the **no-see-ums** were driving me nuts. When I got back to camp everybody was already sacked out to get away from the no-see-ums. I grabbed my MUSKOL repellent first; then rummaged around for a quick snack and did the same. As I climbed in my sleeping bag, thousands of tree frogs, crickets, and several other noisy "night singers" were in full voice in a wonderful chorus. It was sleep inducing (for me anyway); so quickly I fell into deep sleep. The guys mentioned the next morning that they had heard several sturgeon jumping during the night.

Though we had more mosquitoes here than at any of our other campsites, they were not nearly as bothersome as the no-see-ums. The mosquitoes probably were worse here due to the campsite being heavily wooded. But after using my MUSKOL, they left me alone.

NOTE . . .

To those who might not recognize the term "NO-SEE-UMs," to the best of my knowledge, no-see-ums are found only around the outer coastal areas of the lower east coast and Florida. Generally only around salt water and sand. I have never heard of them being more than twenty or thirty miles inland from saltwater. However, they could be in other areas I'm not aware of. A NO-SEE-UM is a tiny insect (as the name implies) so small that you can't see them. Some call them **sandflies,** or **sand gnats.** *They bite like fire;* the itch is unbearable; and unfortunately, the itch and swelling can last for several days. They can drive you wild! They are usually present in swarms. Since you can't see them, they are *extremely* aggravating. In my opinion, they are far more irritating than mosquitoes. Fortunately - they are only bad at certain times of the year! However, a good *high-percent Deet* insect repellent generously applied will usually keep them at bay.

### SIXTEENTH DAY . . . Friday, May 1st
### LAST DAY!

We didn't need an alarm clock in ***this*** campground. A couple of hours before daylight we got our wake up call from the roosters in camp. Each one trying to outdo the other with the loudest call. Needless to say, we were up early again. After a hot shower to get awake and a good breakfast, we were on the water and heading for the Gulf at **7:45 AM.** The air was crystal clear, dead still, and the water like glass. It was a gorgeous morning! The smell of the fresh clean air, the bright and clear sunny morning, gave us all a feeling of euphoria. This was the last day of our trip and all agreed we hated to end it. But we were glad to get started since the NO-SEE-UMS were out in force! Apparently they were only bad in the wooded area, for after a few minutes on the river, they disappeared! Strange! But <u>very</u> welcome!

A gorgeous morning, clear as a bell, no wind, water like glass. What a great day.
(Harry and Ray)  Again Ray said "It don't get any better than this." We agreed!

### FOWLER'S BLUFF!

We arrived at FOWLER's BLUFF at **9:40 AM.** It's a small settlement on the left bank of the SUWANNEE, exactly 13 miles up river from the town of SUWANNEE. Suwannee is situated at the mouth of the river, at the GULF. Fowler's Bluff has a good ramp, and there is a store, named **"SID'S TREASURE CAMP,"** within 50 feet of the ramp. (Phone number in back.) FOWLER'S BLUFF is a very well known historical site. This is a story all of its own. (See the story of **Pirate's Treasure and Gold** on page 86.)

There is a river mileage sign here located _next to the ramp_ that states it is "18 miles to the city of SUWANNEE." This is **incorrect.** By our map information we had calculated 13 more miles, but when we pulled up to the ramp we were surprised to see "18 miles" on the sign. When we went into the store, the owner told us the sign was incorrect, it was only **13** miles. We breathed a sigh of relief. I called THE CANOE OUTPOST, telling them where we were and our ETA in the town of SUWANNEE. I estimated we would arrive at SUWANNEE around **3 PM.**

An unwelcome head-wind came up and we noticed we were working harder than usual and making very little headway. At the time we had no idea we were experiencing a tidal influence. We noticed that the strong current that we had been told to expect, appeared to be absolutely still. It didn't dawn on us what was happening until we got to SUWANNEE and spoke with the locals. However, we managed to arrive in SUWANNEE at exactly **3:15 PM**. By that time we were _"wellspent"_ but were pleased that we had managed to make it reasonably close to our ETA. We had no sooner pulled in and were just stretching our legs when David of the CANOE OUTPOST pulled up. He had driven over 80 miles and arrived within 5 minutes of our arrival. **Great timing!**

At Suwannee, you turn north into a wide canal. At the far end you will see Miller's Marina. The pull-out ramp is immediately behind the large white building.

## MILLER'S MARINA

As I said, we hadn't known about the tide, so I'm alerting you here of this possible problem. We could have spent a leisurely *hour or more* relaxing at FOWLER'S BLUFF waiting for the "outgoing tide". Not only would we not had to work so hard, we would have made it in less time. If you are planning on making the **"to the Gulf"** trip, I highly recommend that you do your homework in this area. Having a tide schedule with you would be *very* helpful. If you need information on the tides or campground reservations, call MILLER'S MARINA.

Thinking back, we still had good current with us when we arrived at YELLOW JACKET the day before . . . so we didn't notice any tide then . . . however, more than likely, we were paddling with an outgoing tide and didn't know it.

It was a superb trip and a wonderful experience. This is one of the greatest flat water rivers I have canoed! Because of the strong current, one of the easiest, and one of the prettiest. Especially from **WHITE SPRINGS** to the **SPIRIT OF THE SUWANNEE** Campground. We unanimously agreed we would love to do it again someday.

We couldn't complain one bit about the weather. It had been absolutely perfect. Out of the 16 days we spent on the trip, that one night at the SANTA FE RIVER was the only bad weather we encountered. A little windy in some places, but that's part of the program.

I wish you smooth water,
and may the wind always be at your back.

Bill Logan

## NOTES

_____

_____

_____

_____

_____

_____

_____

_____

_____

_____

_____

_____

_____

_____

_____

_____

_____

## SUMMARY OF TRIP DISTANCES, AND RIVER TIMES

Again, we were retirees taking our time, stopping several times a day to stretch and 30 to 45 minutes for lunch. **YOUR** times probably will be less. In laying out your trip, if you estimate 2.5 to 3 MPH, you will probably be very close.

### FIRST LEG OF TRIP!
### FARGO TO SPIRIT OF THE SUWANNEE CAMPGROUND
### FOUR AND A HALF DAYS *(OUR TIME)*
(Note . . . **F/F** indicates **F**ROM **F**ARGO)

**DAY ONE**
Left FARGO . . . **10 AM** Left late due to canoe leak.
Pulled out just north of Anderson's Island @ **4:15 PM**
6 hrs. river time.

**DAY TWO**
Left Camp @ **9 AM**
Arrived at Hwy. 6 bridge @ **2 PM** . . . (5 hrs.)
Time from FARGO . . . 11 hrs. . . . 21 Miles!
Pulled out for the night @ **4:30 PM**
7.5 hrs. day river time / 13.5 total hrs. river time, F/F

**DAY THREE**
Left camp @ **8 AM**
Arrived @ CONE BRIDGE @ **9 AM** (14.5 total)
Arrived @ BIG SHOALS @ **12:30 PM**
4.5 hrs. day river time / 18 hrs. total river time F/F

**DAY FOUR**
Left BIG SHOALS @ **9:30 AM**
Pulled out for night @ **3:30 PM** (roughly half way
        between Hwy. 75 and the shoals)
6 hrs. day river time / 24 hrs. total river time F/F

**DAY FIVE . . . END OF FIRST LEG!**
Left camp @ **8:30 AM**
Arrived @ Hwy. 75 @ **11 AM** (2.5 hrs.)
Arrived @ SPIRIT OF THE SUWANNEE @ **1:15 PM**
5 hrs. day river time / 29 hrs. total river time . . . 64 miles F/F

**SIXTH DAY — LAY OVER**
Rest, wash clothes, re-organize, re-supply, etc.
        in LIVE OAK, at Spirit of the Suwannee Campground.

**SEVENTH DAY**
Left campsite @ **10 AM**
Arrived @ Hwy. 249 bridge @ **3 PM** . . . 5 hrs.
Passed SUWANNEE RIVER STATE PARK about **4:30 PM**
Arrived @ campsite on WITHLACOOCHEE @ **5:45 PM**
19.4 miles . . . 7 hrs. 45 min. day river time
36 hrs. 45 min. total F/F

**EIGHTH DAY**
Left camp @ **8:15 AM**
Passed under Hwy. 90 bridge @ **8:25 AM**
Arrived @ DOWLING PARK @ **3:30 PM**
16.8 miles . . . 7 hrs. 15 min. day river time
44 hrs. total river time F/F

**NINTH DAY**
Left DOWLING PARK @ **8 AM**
Arrived @ LAFAYETTE BLUE SPRINGS @ **3 PM**
11 miles . . . 7 hrs. day river time. (bucked heavy wind)
58 total river time F/F

**TENTH DAY**
Left LAFAYETTE BLUE SPRINGS @ **8 AM**
Arrived at abandoned camp on right, @ **3 PM**
19 miles . . . 7 hrs. day river time
58 total river time F/F
**ELEVENTH DAY . . . SUNDAY**
*Stayed put to avoid the heavy pleasure craft traffic.*
**TWELFTH DAY . . . BRANFORD! END OF SECOND LEG!**
Left camp @ **7:30 AM**
Arrived TROY SPRINGS @ **8:20**
Arrived LITTLE RIVER SPRINGS @ **9 AM**
Arrived BRANFORD @ **10:30 AM** (9 miles) Re-supplied!
Left BRANFORD @ **11:30 AM**
Arrived at campsite across from SANTA FE RIVER @ **4 PM**
20 miles . . . 7.5 day river time (incl. - 1 hr.)
65.5 total hrs. river time F/F
**THIRTEENTH DAY**
*Stayed put to dry out from storm the night before.*
**FOURTEENTH DAY**
Left camp @ **8 AM**
Arrived @ ROCK BLUFF @ Hwy. 340 @ **11 AM**
Re-supplied at store, lunch and left @ **12:15**
Re-tracked to ROCK BLUFF SPRINGS @ **12:35 PM**
Left ROCK BLUFF SPRINGS @ **1 PM**
Passed GUARANTO SPRINGS CAMPGROUND @ **1:30 PM**
Pulled out at WANNEE for about 20 minutes
Arrived at SUN SPRINGS @ **4 PM** (EULA LANDING)
Ate supper there and left @ **5 PM**
Arrived @ HART SPRINGS @ **5:45 PM**
Arrived @ OLDTOWN Suwannee Gables Motel @ **11 PM**
15 hrs. river time, less 3 hrs. = 12 hrs. day river time
30 miles total covered . . . 77.5 total river time F/F
**FIFTEENTH DAY**
Left OLDTOWN @ **8:15 AM**
Arrived @ FANNIN SPRINGS @ **8:30 AM**
Left FANNIN SPRINGS @ **8:45 AM**
Arrived @ MANATEE SPRINGS @ **12 Noon**
Lunch, relax and enjoyed the park – Left @ **2 PM**
Arrived @ YELLOW JACKET Camp @ **3:30 PM**
7 hrs. 15 min. less 2 hrs. 15 min. = 5 hrs. day river time
13 miles . . . 5 hrs.   82.5 miles total river time F/F
**SIXTEENTH DAY — LAST DAY OF TRIP!**
Left YELLOW JACKET @ **7:45 AM**
Arrived @ FOWLER'S BLUFF @ **9:40 AM**
Left FOWLER'S BLUFF @ **10:15 AM**
Arrived in the town of SUWANNEE @ **3:15 PM**
7 hrs. daily river time . . . 19 river miles

TOTAL RIVER MILES TRAVELED — **213**

TOTAL RIVER TIME FROM FARGO — **89.5 HOURS**
ROUGHLY 2.37 MPH

## CAMPGROUND INFORMATION

If you plan on putting in **at** the **OKEFENOKEE SWAMP;** you can launch from the marina in **STEPHEN FOSTER REC. PARK** campground. Camping, **$12.00** night, includes water and electric in all sites. They also have a large group site. Launch fee $1.00 — For day use, sign out at Marina office, you must be out of the swamp and signed back in by 6:00 PM. You cannot camp inside the swamp anywhere without a permit. Canoe trails are generally well marked. NO pets are allowed at any time. This is probably due to attracting 'gators. Streets are all paved and there are roughly 55 sites and 7 very nice cabins. However, to get one, you need reservations *FAR* in advance. There are handicapped facilities and "RV only" campsites. Clean restrooms with showers and plenty of hot water. When we left on our trip, the "sill" *was* closed so we were not able to launch from there though that was our original plan. The "sill" is *now open* and that route is now possible. ("Sill" . . . a small earthen dam at the southwest corner of the swamp, but easy to get over.) Don't forget, to go over the sill you'll need a permit from Park Headquarters.

If you prefer to put in at the outer edge of the swamp; just *below the Sill;* you can put in at **GRIFFIS' FISH CAMP** on the same road **(HWY. 177)** as STEPHEN FOSTER REC. PARK; on the left about 3 miles *before* the park. Good sandy launch area and wooded campsites w/Ramada's **($8.00** site + $2 extra person over two). $2.00 launch fee.

If you put in at FARGO, there is a large sand bar, just east of the bridge to camp on overnight before launching. **IF** . . . the water is not too high. Small restaurant and grocery one block north. If the water is high, and there is no place to camp, call the Sheriff (number in back) and explain. They probably will allow you to camp in the picnic area the night before you launch.

If you wish to follow the **"UPPER FLORIDA CANOE TRAIL,"** it starts at **Hwy. 6 bridge.** There is an adequate area for overnight camping on the northwest side of the bridge (only). It has a sloping sandy beach to launch. The Canoe Trail ends at Suwannee River State Park about 15 miles below Live Oak.

**"SPIRIT OF THE SUWANNEE"** Campground is beautifully wooded and **extremely well manicured.** They have paved streets, superb tent camping (with tables) as well as super RV sites that will accommodate the largest of RVs. They have it all; large clean restrooms, showers, cabins, laundry, restaurant, and fantastic gospel and country music shows. Large grassy fields for baseball, football or soccer. Large play area for kids. And a huge amphitheater where some of the *biggest names* in **country and gospel music** come to perform here. And of course . . . **THE CANOE OUTPOST** is located on the grounds, at the river. I highly recommend it. (Tents **$12.00** per, w/water and electric.) Lots of pay phones.

**SUWANNEE RIVER STATE PARK** with 1800 acres is a very large park and has two large picnic pavilions. On its grounds are located old Civil War encampments, and what is believed to be the oldest cemetery in the state of Florida. The Park is on both sides of the river. It has 31 campsites, a ramp, pay phone, and picnic areas. It is the lower pull out point for the (upper) **FLORIDA CANOE TRAIL.** They have nice hiking trails, on both sides of the river. It is very clean and very pretty here. Pets are not allowed in the camping areas; except for service dogs. In other areas they must be on a leash at all times. It is located 13 miles west of Live Oak, off Hwy. 90. Though we did not camp here on our trip, I came back here several months later! For more info, call 904-362-2746.

**LAFAYETTE BLUE SPRINGS,** has good tent camping with tables and fresh water piped to the sites; large restrooms and hot showers. Cold sodas and candies etc. Excellent swimming area. Good sandy place to pull your canoes out. $10.00 per site.

**OLDTOWN KOA** — This is a fancy campground. It has just about everything: 100 RV sites, tent sites, pool, recreation room, laundry, volleyball, basketball, ramp, gasoline, camping, cabins, and a small store. Tent sites are $16.00; however, they are not close to the river.

**MANATEE SPRINGS PARK** is 23 miles from the Gulf. It covers 2,075 acres. A beautiful park catering to campers, picnicking, swimming, canoeing and fishing, hiking and biking on 8.5 miles of winding trails. There are 86 campsites, no cabins; and has a concession stand. Pets are not allowed in the camping areas. This is a great place to bring the family. The spring gushes a whopping 116 million gallons of crystal clear water a day at a constant temperature of 72 degrees. (This is a correction . . . We were told 109 million when we were there.) It also has a nice dock for power boat users that protrudes out into the Suwannee about fifty feet. Those areas of trails that are over swampy ground have nicely raised boardwalks. Two tents per site limit. Camping fee: **$10.00** - 65 or older or disabled, $5.00. Add $2.00 for electric - $2.00 for each person over four. Alcoholic beverages and firearms are not permitted.

**YELLOW JACKET CAMPGROUND.** Cabins, tent sites, restrooms and hot showers. Sandy canoe landing. In a very pretty wooded area. **$10.00** per site (2 people) - $2.00 each for over two.

**FOWLER'S BLUFF.** As I said, there is no regular campground here. I spoke with the owner of the grocery by phone at this writing and he told me in the past when confronted with inclement weather; canoers have been allowed to camp there. If you are so inclined, they also have cabins to rent and a picnic area with tables. There is also a good ramp, a pay phone on the porch of the store, and the store has miscellaneous supplies.

**"MILLER'S MARINE" CAMPGROUND,** in the town of **SUWANNEE!** A few tent sites behind the big white building, with a good ramp and pay phone. There is a **superb** restaurant within walking distance. Campsite fee **$12.00.** Be *sure* to have your repellent with you if the "NO-SEE-UMS" are in season.

**SOME OF THESE PRICES MAY CHANGE!**
**BEST TO CALL!**

## CANOE CAMPING SUGGESTED CHECK LIST
### Make your own list. Adjust to your preferences.

Wide brim **hat,**
**Sunscreen,**
**Sunglasses,** (with lanyard). Without a lanyard, I can almost guarantee you will lose them over the side.
**Rain Gear** - Do not buy the cheap stuff. Buy only the best. There is nothing more miserable that being wet and cold all day.
**Insect repellent.** I have tried many and found "Muskol" to work best. HOWEVER, SEE WARNING ON PAGE 79.
**Eating and cooking utensils.** When space and weight are my primary concern I use my old "GI" stainless mess kit. Wal-Mart also has "Lexan" knives and forks. Feather light - extremely strong.
**Cook stove** - whatever kind you use, don't forget spare fuel if extended trip.
Insulated(?) **Coffee mug or** light plastic drinking cup.
**Paper towels.**
Several **changes of clothing.** Don't forget, you'll need extra socks and dry shoes.
**Wet and dry shoes** - Slip-on sneaker type deck shoes are good. I like diver's wet suit boots for my wet shoes. Checkout the sandals called "River Rapids" sold by Wal-Mart. Waterproof, very _inexpensive_, adjustable, indestructible, comfortable.
**Tent** - Re-waterproof before leaving. A 6 mil. visquene **ground cloth** works great and no weight.
Good **sleeping bag** of proper weight for weather. Also, a self inflating type mattress pad well worth the money.
**Light Jacket or sweater** if cool. Also a couple of different weight shirt changes. Maybe a sweatshirt.
If you think you might blister - try the **"cut-off" gloves.** No fingers. Golfing gloves are also good but pricey.
**Cooler** - (If you feel you must take one.) Most "pro" campers take only those items that do not require ice. However, if you are one of those who enjoy a "cool beverage," now and then (as I do) then here is the way to do it. If you want your ice to last three times longer, adhere closely to the following and you will _easily do so_ . . . **IF** . . . you are using a good quality name brand cooler. Pre-chill your cooler (if you can) and items, starting two to three days before leaving. Use only **"Block Ice."** If you have a large

freezer and the room, put your block ice AND cooler in the freezer and crank the temperature down to its lowest point. WHY? When you purchase any ice, it is barely cold enough to keep it frozen. By bringing your ice down to 0-5 degrees, you extend the time it takes to melt considerable. (Consider making your own.) I fill 1/3 of my small cooler with water and put it in the freezer three days ahead. That way the ice is solid. You **must keep the cooler out of direct sunlight.** Cover it well with pieces of clothing or (?). I use clothing underneath a folded silver **space blanket** - with a towel or (?) _on top of it_ to keep the glare out of my eyes. It will reflect most of the heat. Good idea to also stuff insulating items around the sides also. If your trip is an extended one, and you want ice for most of the trip, there is an even more effective way to extend it even further. Put a good size piece of dry ice (wrapped well in newspaper) on top of your ice. Keep the newspaper over your ice _even after it is wet_ and the dry ice is gone. It will still do a great job of insulating. I also put a small hand towel over the top of the newspaper. Even wet it keeps the heat away from the ice. _Especially if the newspaper is still there also._ Believe me, this will really extend your ice **much** longer. However, you **MUST** keep your cooler away from heat no matter which method you use. As an example of the above efficiency, a group of us took a 5-day trip. I used the freezer and dry ice method. At the end of the trip **I still had 60% of my original block of ice 5 days later.** Everyone else had no ice by the end of the third day. Experiment - you may even be able to better this. If you use dry ice - **do not** put anything against it that will rupture when frozen.

**Life Jacket** - Wear it - don't use it for a cushion. Good idea to secure a whistle to it.

**Folding Chair** - (optional). After being in a canoe for 8 hours or more, you will rejoice at relaxing in a good folding chair. It's light, compact, easy to secure on top of your gear with bungee cords.

**A Good Sharp Knife** - is a must. You don't need a "Jim Bowie" monster. All you need is a good sturdy sharp blade.

**Wood cutting tool.** Some prefer a hatchet. I prefer a good sharp machete. Light, packs easy (in a sheath).

**Food** - for how many days you plan on being away . . . then add two extra days for an emergency should you be caught in inclement weather and have to stay put until it clears. A few items that are great for a long trip: **Bagels** are the answer for bread. They keep well and are almost indestructible. **Pepperoni** keeps without ice and makes a great lunch or dinner snack with Ritz crackers. I found that the almost 2 inch roll has far better flavor than the 1 inch roll and is not nearly as greasy when warm. **Parmalat** is a superb substitute for milk. It does not require refrigeration and the taste is "almost" as good as milk. Get the pints. Not quarts. It has shelf life – check dates.

**Flashlight** - if extended trip, extra batteries. I like "Miners type" light on a headband. Keeps both hands free.

**First Aid Kit** - small one to cover cuts, abrasions, sunburn, headache, upset stomach, etc. No big kit necessary.

**Extra Paddle** - NEVER go out without a spare paddle and secure it well *inside* your canoe.

**One Gallon of Fresh Water** per person - per day - is standard. Adjust according to your needs. Just remember it weighs **8 lbs. per gallon.** Best to take many small containers than one large (easier to evenly distribute weight). Refill often.

**5 Gallon Buckets** with tight lids make great water and animal proof containers. They also double as stools, tables, etc. The plastic ones (like bird seed) are lighter. If you use several - color code tops for ID.

**Canoe Bow Painter.** (Bow line.) You should have a fairly long one. Twenty feet best . . . but no less than fifteen. Some places you will need long lines to tie up. Stern line is also useful but not mandatory. Same length.

**Camera and/or Camcorder** - Whichever you use, make certain you have plenty of film **_AND_** spare batteries.

**Heavy Mil. Large Garbage Bags** - to double bag your gear in case of heavy rain. At least a dozen.

If you plan to fish, take only **one rod** and a very small amount of your best lures. NOT a full tackle box.

**Common plastic grocery bags** . . . for trash you will carry out. Better the small ones than the large. They distribute and store better. Don't overfill them and tie tops tightly.

**Most important item! Latrine!** Camping and hiking over the years, I guess I have tried about everything. The best, easiest to pack, and the least amount of trouble is: Two small canvas top camp type - folding stools with a 4 foot 2x4 laid between them. It is almost a luxury item. The older you are the more you will appreciate this.

**Small Folding Shovel** - for digging your latrine or whatever else. You do not need anything large. **But,** PLEASE DO NOT BURY YOUR TRASH – CARRY IT OUT WITH YOU. And last - **Toilet paper.** Put it *inside a coffee can with a lid.* That way it will stay dry even in the heaviest of dew or rain. If you don't have a coffee can, place the roll upright on a cut off stick – pull a zip-lock bag down over it.

**Note** - Everyone has a tendency to take more than they need. *We all do!* If you prefer to travel light, assemble everything in one place prior to leaving. *Go over it several times* making sure what you are taking will be used. Remember, cans and bottles are heavy and will need to be brought out. Freeze dried backpacking foods are the lightest, least amount of trash, and take up the least amount of space. However, be sure you have at least two days more food than you need. But do not *underestimate your needs.* The best way to do that is to package *each meal separately.* Keep your munchies, like trail mix or whatever, in a separate container and handy to you in your canoe. I keep my lunch snacks in a second container (the PVC tube) also handy when we pull out for a break.

## NOTES

_____

_____

_____

_____

_____

_____

_____

_____

_____

_____

_____

## OTHER ITEMS OF INTEREST

Several items such as **MUSKOL** repellent, **LANACANE** to stop the itch, and **IVY DRY** for Poison Ivy . . . are in my opinion, excellent products. I arrived at my decision from trial and error over 40 years of camping. (See phone numbers.)

Use whatever you like best, but I urge you to put these items to a field test and compare them with your favorite product. I think you will determine, as I have, that most of the above products will generally outperform others. I will warn you here, however, that Muskol on your hands will damage *some* plastics. Using care, test this for yourself. That way you will never have a problem in this area. Washing your hands before handling plastic items is prudent with any repellant.

**WARNING – All repellants**. High concentrations of Deet have been found to be dangerous to <u>very</u> <u>young</u> children. There have been cases of severe allergic reaction. Consult your physician or pharmacist before using on small children.

On the subject of performance, I recently discovered **BULLFROG sun block.** It was recommended to me by my doctor as we were discussing my upcoming trip. I used it every morning on this trip and though I was in the sun ALL DAY . . . for 13 days of the trip . . . I didn't even have the slightest bit of pink, much less a burn. I am *very* fair skinned and burn easily. It was **superb** . . . so I recommend it to anyone who is fair skinned and doesn't want to ruin their trip with a sunburn.

If you can get your *refills* of water from the head of the spring, right where it comes out of the ground, I would have no qualms about drinking it "as is." I definitely recommend you **DO NOT** drink any water directly from the river without first **boiling it** for at least 5 minutes. With as many springs as there are around the river, you should *never* have a problem with drinking water. *(Unless* you are canoeing at very high water.) I did not see **any** springs on the first leg of the trip; but you shouldn't need water there anyway.

A 4" dia. x 24" (or whatever length suits you) piece of **PVC** pipe (get the one **called sewer pipe)** . . . it's lighter . . . any plumbing supply shop will cut you whatever size you want . . . and it is *VERY inexpensive.* Add a PVC "cap" to each end, and you have an excellent animal proof food container. It also floats and is compact and it packs easily. I use one for my Pepperoni and Ritz cracker lunch snacks, etc. Both of those items are very odorous and animals are attracted to them. In the PVC I never have to worry about animals getting into them. Even 'coons or wild hogs. *And* they are semi-waterproof.

While you are at the plumbing supply, pick up one **3' length** of 7/8 pipe **insulation.** Where you rest your legs or knees against the sides of the canoe, glue a 12 inch piece of this insulation. It will do **WONDERS** for your comfort on a long trip. I found it necessary to first glue a split piece of garden hose on the rail, then glue the piece of insulation over it. Otherwise, the insulation will not hold by itself.

## ANOTHER TIP

If you *do not* use a **Rod Protector tube** for your fishing rods: On recent trips I have found that a 4" PVC tube with a cap on the bottom only. Drill two small holes on the open end, side by side. Attach permanently one end of a 1/8 bungee cord to one of the holes. This makes a great "scabbard" to hold several rods and reels. I put the bottom end pointed forward and on the bottom of the canoe. The top rests on one of my thwarts. With the hard PVC I no longer have to worry about my rods getting broken or my eyelets smashed. Put the rods inside the tube, then wrap the bungee around at the reel *stands;* put the hook in the second small hole. With this setup, I can remove a rod at anytime. Also, you don't have to worry about the rods getting snagged on brush, getting broken or falling over the side. Again, get the *'sewer pipe' . . . it's lighter* than regular PVC.

I mentioned Gatorade since it stores well, keeps well, is excellent for replenishing your electrolytes, easy to mix, and has a pleasant taste. Soda pop is heavy, bulky to pack, requires ice and when you are out in the sun for long periods, tends to make one **more thirsty.** Also then you have a can that must be carried out. The package the Gatorade comes in is burnable.

## MORE USEFUL PRODUCTS

MUSKOL repellent mentioned several places is not in all stores. It is sometimes hard to find but most sporting goods stores carry it. It is extremely efficient. If you have trouble finding it, it can also be purchased directly from Schrins-Plough, Inc., P.O. Box 337, Memphis, TN 38151. A 10-oz. bottle is $3.75 - Aerosol is $4.18 - The pump spray is 1.25-oz. **and is 100% Deet** for $4.30 – this *includes* shipping. Request **"100% Deet!"** I have been canoeing in the Boundary Waters of Northern Minnesota in the early summer on lakes where the mosquitoes were to thick you could kill a half dozen just by slapping your hands together. After applying MUSKOL, I was bite-free for 6 to 8 hours. The buzzing around my ears was still a nuisance, but they didn't bite.

While on the subject of bites and itches, I have found over the years for an itchy insect bite (including "NO-SEE-UMS") the best thing for me is "LANACANE!" It stops the itch in seconds. At least for me anyway. For POISON IVY . . . I prefer "IVY-DRY", available in most drug stores. It dries up the blisters fast (but does not stop the itching). Use LANACANE for that after the application dries. Works great! However, to be certain you do not have an allergy to any of these products, especially the 100% Deet, you should *check with your family physician . . . or at least your pharmacist. *

## A LITTLE SOMETHING ABOUT CANOES

Canoeing is a *quiet fun*, sometimes very exciting, family recreation accessible to almost any area of the U.S. Canoers often camp plus commune with nature and wildlife. Hopefully, the following information on buying a canoe or renting for an occasional canoe trip will be helpful to the beginner.

**Buying a canoe is easy . . . right?** *Not necessarily.* You need to think about where and how you will use it the *most.* Will you use it for lake trips, rivers, or wilderness pack trips? For flat water or for white water? Almost any canoe will get you where you are going (except for whitewater); you need to think carefully about your needs before you buy. A good analogy is what you need to get to work. A bicycle, a motorcycle, a sports car, a sedan or pickup. Though every one of them *would get you there*, you would pick the one that suits your needs the best. *Canoes are no different.*

**Lake Canoes . . .** Speed will be helped somewhat by a slightly rounded bottom, however, it will also be more tipsy. A **small keel** is desirable to lessen side wind drift. The **bow** and **stern** should be low to offer less wind resistance. If you will be carrying several people a little higher **freeboard** is desirable. Also you need one that has a higher load capacity. Load capacity of a canoe is determined by the U.S. Coast Guard by loading a canoe down until it has 6 inches of freeboard. It will be stamped on the canoe's ID plate.

**Wilderness Canoe** requirements are almost the same as above except you need cargo space. Load capacity is important. Most common are the sixteen to eighteen footers. Though a keel is desirable, it is not essential since you will be carrying more weight and are not as easily blown off course. Ease of paddling and control is more important than speed. Durability is more important. One *very important* factor is weight. Though a heavy canoe might not be as noticeable on the water, when you go to portage, it will do you in . . . fast. Get the lightest, most durable one you can find. You should also have a yoke for carrying especially if you will be traveling alone. The new "Royalex" canoes are great for strength, durability and are **super light.** *But . . . can also be quite pricey!*

**River Canoe . . .** Again, like both of the above in many ways, but the bow and stern flare is higher, to keep out splashing water. Some rocker is also desirable. (Rocker is, on the bottom, the bow and the stern are raised slightly from the center of the canoe. Each manufacturer has their own idea how much is best for different classes of whitewater. (Best to ASK!) A keel is definitely NOT desirable! You need to have all the control you can get. A keel in this case can be caught by the side swirls and current and can make your canoe harder to maneuver.

A rounded bottom is much more desirable. Strength and durability are the most important factors. Best length for solo is thirteen to fifteen feet, and tandem sixteen to seventeen. Several manufacturers offer 14s. If you are going to use it in true whitewater, it is best that you have a good *strong cover* to keep out water. It must be extremely well fastened. Should it suddenly give way in a chute, you could find yourself in serious trouble. If you plan on getting serious and running whitewater often, ,you might want to look into the special boots (or skirt) made for that purpose. Or by fabricating a super light kevlar or (?) decking. The best idea is to *fill all empty areas* with flotation such as **Dagger's** special *whitewater* **"Open Canoe Flotation"** bags. Mohawk has them also. There are any number of good materials for a canoe. Naturally, the best material is also the most expensive. Among the most used are Kevlar, Fiberglass, Aluminum, and the newer technology materials such as Royalite, and Royalex. Also, **Dagger** now has a new material called R-Light, an ABS plastic material, and another called EXL they are using in both their canoes and kayaks.

There are dozens of good canoe makers out there. The ones I like and have proven track records are, **Dagger, Old Town and the new Mohawk.** Since the Suwannee trip, three of the regulars in our canoe group have bought Mohawk's **"Blazer 16"** and swear by them. I can attest that they are *very* **FAST** and extremely easy to maneuver! *I have a hard time keeping up with them.* If you are buying a fast water canoe, don't forget to include in your pack; material to make repairs should you sustain serious damage on a whitewater river. And of course . . . that extra paddle!

**On the subject of paddles:** When buying a paddle, you want to get the strongest, yet the *lightest* one you can find. Weight is **the** most important factor. You could be paddling for hours and hours at roughly 15-20 strokes per minute. If you buy a cheap paddle that weights a ton, you will soon tire and then each stroke becomes work. That will ruin a trip quick.

**Buying a paddle also needs some thought.** A paddle too short, too long or too heavy *is the pits.* You should buy a paddle that when the tip is resting on the floor, the handle is even with your nose. Also, get a good quality one, not a cheap one. Remember, not only will you use this paddle for many years to come, your life might depend on its strength some day should you suddenly get into a dangerous situation.

**What kind should I buy?** There are all kinds of paddles on the market. You should choose the one that fits your needs the best. It could be the traditional wood, or it could be plastic and metal or one of the newer high tech composite paddles. Many years ago, paddles were only wood and were relatively low cost. Today, a good high quality wood paddle will cost you a pretty penny. The everyday "featherlite and off the rack" wood paddle is still a good choice and it can be purchased for a reasonable amount. But if you have one custom made, be prepared for a shock. They can be quite pricey. The main advantage of the wood paddle is it's light, looks and feels great. The disadvantage is that it requires a lot of maintenance. Both varnish and wax. Those who are very particular use a hard wax extra protection.

The biggest advantage of the metal loomed and plastic blade paddle is that you can use it forever without doing anything more than keeping it clean and stored in a reasonable environment. I personally use both the metal plastic and the wood. Which type I use depends on the circumstances of my trip. Some people use the double (kayak type) paddles. They seem to work fine. However, if you get into some narrow places like you might find in the Okefenokee Swamp, I personally believe it would be more trouble than it's worth. However, I'm told out in the open they work great.

Also, get the type grip (top) that feels comfortable to you. There are four or five different types of grips. Try several. I prefer the "T" handle. It gives me better control and I find it suits my needs best. (It also functions well as a boat hook if needed.) It is only available on the metal-plastic and composite models. Not in wood. At least I have never seen one on wood. I doubt seriously if it would stay together with much use. My metal-plastics have the "T" handle. My wood featherlites have the one depicted below in the sketch. Some call it a wedge. I'm not sure that is the correct name.

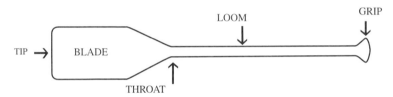

The *average* width of a paddle blade runs around six to eight inches. Custom Racing paddles can be purchased with blades as wide as you want. Some racers use blades as wide as 10 to 12 inches. There is also a sweet wooden paddle on the market called a "Bent Paddle." I tried it and love it. However, they are not cheap. I found it to be _extremely efficient_ and easy to use. Someday, I would like to own a custom-made wooden one of these with a nine-inch blade. (They are also made in metal-plastic.)

## IMPORTANT PARTS OF A CANOE

Below are some descriptions that hopefully will be helpful in discussing your needs with a dealer.

A. BEAM
B. DEPTH
C. DRAFT
D. FREEBOARD
E. TUMBLEHOME
F. WIDTH AT GUNWALES
    (pronounced gunnels.)

F. Only to determine the maximum width of objects when loading, fitting a cover, or ? etc.

Tumblehome - the amount of angle (curvature) the canoe has between the beam and the gunwales.

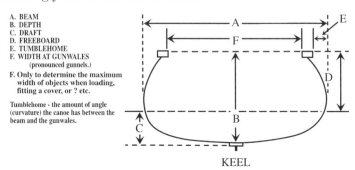

### What are canoe lines?

The lines of a canoe really mean the overall shape of the canoe. To a large degree the shape will determine how the canoe handles. A narrow canoe will cut through the water faster than a wide beam canoe, and a canoe with a straight flat bottom will add speed to your paddling. The ability to turn depends on the amount of rocker exhibited by the canoe. Rocker again is the amount of curvature along the line of the keel line of the canoe from one end to the other. Canoes with a lot of rocker are very maneuverable in fast water, however, they are serious work to maneuver on flat water.

The bottom shape of the canoe as viewed end-on will determine both stability and speed. A canoe with a flat bottom while being the most stable on flat water, will be somewhat sluggish to paddle. Faster canoes are rounded on the bottom, however, they are also more easily tipped.

The shapes of the sides of the canoe will determine the ease of paddling and its seaworthiness. Canoes with a lot of tumblehome (curvature of the sides) to the sides are most efficient as the paddle can be brought closer to the keel line. However, tumblehome can be a disadvantage in rough water as water tends to be deflected *into* the canoe.

Flared sides tent to deflect the water away from the canoe. However, paddling with flared sides is not near as efficient and a canoe flared through the center section can be difficult to paddle solo.

Straight sided canoes offer a feeling of predictability as the canoe is leaned over. They offer secondary stability (the stability of the canoe as it leaves a level position) than a canoe with tumblehome.

**Length and width . . .** The length of the canoe in general will determine the speed. Generally, the longer the canoe, the faster it will go for the same amount of effort. However, the speed of the canoe will also depend on the weight and the lines of the canoe. Canoe length will also determine its carrying capacity and handling.

In general, shorter canoes will turn more easily than longer canoes. Wider canoes are more stable than narrow ones, however, again speed is sacrificed for stability and ease of maneuvering. A wider canoe will have more carrying capacity which is a feature that must be considered if you will be using it for long distance trips.

*The following copyrighted article was reprinted with authorization from Terry Jensen of Cybersports. Their e-mail address is listed at the end of their article.*

### Buying a Canoe

Before actually purchasing a canoe or kayak, it pays to consider what type would be best for you to own. Once the only canoe available was made of wood and bark. Then the bark was replaced by canvas stretched over a frame of wooden ribs (usually cedar), and planks. Wood/canvas canoes lead the market until the end of World War II, when the aluminum canoe was born. This was the beginning of various materials used to construct canoes. Construction now varies from fiberglass and plastic to contemporary fibers.

Wooden canoes, while traditional, are time and labor intensive, making them very expensive. In addition, they are also the most fragile and are certainly not suitable for white water. Traditionalists might consider purchasing a wood canoe kit for the fun of building it and to cut the cost of a traditional canoe.

Aluminum canoes are the most popular of all canoes. Inspired by aircraft technology, they are made from twin halves connected by a keel that has stem plates riveted over a longitudinal seam. Since aluminum is actually too soft for durability, aluminum alloys containing magnesium and silicone are used to add strength to this lightweight metal. Heat-tempered alloys are best. **Aluminum canoes are: Noisy, Lightweight, Durable, Cold in Winter, Hot in Summer.**

The advent of **fiberglass** allowed canoe manufacturers to produce inexpensive, low maintenance canoes. These canoes are made from plastic resin reinforced with fibers of glass and/or other materials. The canoes that are resins used with woven cloth produce a higher quality product with greater tensile strength than mixing short strands of chopped fiber into a plastic resin, then molding. The number of layers and weight of cloth varies from canoe manufacturer to manufacturer as does the type of resin, the weight, amount of labor and materials. When low price is high priority, fiberglass works. Always check the lay-up of the fiber and resin construction to make certain your canoe will be durable.

**Kevlar** canoes are made from a fiber developed by Dupont as a tire cord. Kevlar 49 adds strength both for abrasion and tearing, without weight. It can be punctured, however. Because this fiber is expensive, some companies have experimented with sandwiching layers of fiberglass between two layers of Kevlar to reinforce the hull and reduce the price. Prices vary depending upon the construction.

**Royalex** is the trade name for a styrene material (ABS) made by Uniroyal. Royalex is sandwiched between two layers of vinyl to protect the ABS from ultraviolet light. Canoe companies vacuum wrap the heated material around designs gunwaled with wood or vinyl-covered aluminum. **Canoes made from this process are: Nearly Indestructible, Flexible, Heavy, Slow.** The durability of Royalex canoes make them the most popular for whitewater canoeing.

There are several others which you may wish to look into. The most popular of the new technology materials today being **Royalite.** Similar in strength to the Royalex only lighter. **And** . . . more expensive.

*Submit information about canoes and canoeing via e-mail to:*
**canoe@dfwnetmall.com     (Cybersports)**

---

### Unsure? Rent a Canoe

Unless you canoe often and/or own your own camping gear, you will probably find it more advantageous to contract with a canoe outfitter to organize your trip and equipment. Your canoe liveryman is also a good source of information before buying. However, always get *at least* three *or four* opinions before making up your mind.

---

### FOWLER'S BLUFF
*Reprinted with permission of Sid's Treasure Camp owner,*
*Bill Wise, of Fowler's Bluff, FL*

*I have included this story since (1) I thought you would find it interesting reading, (2) Fowler's Bluff is a stop you will want to make on your trip.*

Fowler's Bluff is home of one of the many mysteries from the days of the Pirates. It is synonymous with Florida's Pirate treasure history. During the 17th through 19th centuries, this area provided camps to some of the most famous pirates of Florida's history.

Around 1820, pirates are believed to have buried three (or more) chests of gold coin and bullion on the banks of the Suwannee River at Fowler's Bluff somewhere behind what is now known as "Sid's Treasure Camp (store). Exactly who buried the treasure is not known, as most Pirates did not keep ships' logs or live long enough to tell their tales.

What is known has been well documented on the pages of such publications as the *Chiefland Citizen* newspaper, the *Gainesville Sun, Tampa Tribune, Saturday Evening Post,* and several books. Over the past 100 years, many men have tried to recover the gold.

In 1897, Emmitt Baird acquired a map showing the location of the chests. Although he never claimed to have recovered any of them, after he left the site, he suddenly became very rich, and started a large hardware store, a bank, and built the "Baird Building" in Gainesville.

Along about 1923, Robert Malone, using some type of metal sensor, confirmed two chests, approximately where the old map showed them to be. Although his crew made contact with one of the chests, it sank deeper into the quicksand that underlies the area. Malone built a steel-plated coffer dam to pump out the quicksand and divers attached a sling to the chest to haul it to the surface. When the cable broke, the chest fell and again disappeared into the quicksand. Funds running out, Malone gave up.

In the 1940's and 1950's, divers again reported seeing the chest but did not have the right technology to bring it to the surface. Jim Theroux, cousin of the world-renown treasure hunter Mel Fisher, and Phil Olin, founded Freshwater Archeology of Alachua in late 1989. Using ground-probing radar, they were able to locate what they thought to be the remaining treasure chests.

After a year of building coffer dams and digging to a depth of 30 feet, the said they only turned up gold shavings, stalactites, battered posts and an underground cave that was too cramped to explore. Quicksand made it too difficult to use large equipment. Theroux said they had done all they could with the technology available at that time so again the treasure eluded being recovered.

All that gold is still down there, just waiting for someone with the right know-how to find it.

As you walk the banks of the Suwannee behind Sid's Treasure Camp Store . . . just imagine — only a few feet under you . . . may lie more Pirate's gold than in your wildest dreams.

## SOME SAFETY AND A FEW COMMON SENSE REMINDERS
*Most of the following is known to all who canoe regularly.*
*However, since this book is aimed mostly at newcomers to canoeing,*
*and first time Suwannee River canoers . . . here's*
*a few basic things I feel important.*

Inexperienced canoers soon find there's a little more to paddling a canoe safely than just carefully sitting in it. We all started at that point. I well remember my first experience in a canoe some 60 years ago at Boy Scout Camp. It was a wet one. So mentally store some of these tips, get a couple of trips under your belt, and you'll soon become an "old pro."

When you buy a canoe from a dealer you should ask how much flotation it has and what kind. Air tanks only filled with foam or? (Some of the newer canoes have foam in their construction.) If you are unsure, the best way to find out is to swamp it in shallow water and check it. I bought two used canoes. On both I refilled the flotation space at each end with styrofoam from a can. This foam can be purchased at any home supply store and is easy to apply. Just drill a 1/4" hole, poke the snout in the hole and press the button. The compartment will be quickly filled and in a few minutes it will harden. You may need two or three cans per end if they are empty. Trim the unsightly mess that oozes out then put a self threading screw in the hole.

**Loading your canoe for a long trip . . .** Load it so that the center of gravity is as low as possible by putting your heaviest pieces to the center bottom. Also, make sure you keep the weight even so that the canoe sits in the water **level** without you in it; *both* sideways and length ways. After you have loaded, it is a good idea to move it away from the bank and check how it is riding. It is also important to remember that the two people (if ?) who will be paddling also need to balance their weight evenly as possible. If one is heavier, he should paddle from the back. When you are in and ready to pull out, your canoe should be now "only slightly" higher in the front.

A few **don'ts . . .**
**Don't** drag your canoe to the water. Pick it up and carry it.
**Don't** overload your canoe. The minimum freeboard, gear
and people is six inches.
**Don't** go out without your life jacket and extra paddle.
**Don't** leave on a trip without someone knowing your
itinerary.
**Don't** pull your canoe up on the bank and leave it without
tying it off also.

**Don't** leave foods in your canoe overnight; especially your cooler.

**Don't** leave your canoe upright when threatened with inclement weather. Turn it upside down. Make certain it is *also* tied down well.

**Don't** leave your paddles in the canoe or on the shore. Take them with you to your tent area.

**Don't** lay your spare paddle loose in your canoe. Best that it is securely tied inside the canoe, but not so tight you can't get to it easy if need be. If not tied and you dump, you could possible lose it.

**Don't** attempt to *river* canoe without getting your feet wet. *Those who try to keep their feet dry usually end up getting their hair wet.* Take sandals or sneakers specifically for water. I prefer an old pair of divers boots. Or - keep a towel and dry shoes and socks handy.

I **DON'T** recommend an inexperienced canoer going on a long river trip for the first time that *does* **not** know how to swim. If they must go along, it should be made *very clear at the beginning* it is **mandatory** they wear their life jacket **at all times** *when* they are on the water. No *exceptions!*

**Don't** horseplay *"on a trip."* It could ruin it for everyone. Canoe horseplay, when out for a day and in your bathing suit is great fun and I wholeheartedly recommend it to everyone; especially kids *(who can swim)*. On the river, I strongly suggest you save it for later.

If you are going to canoe at a *very high* water, **don't** paddle alone. **Use the Buddy System.** This is doubly true if you are planning on paddling the **upper** parts of this river. There are too many trees, overhanging limbs, etc. These are called Strainers. The water can move easily through the limbs and logs but you cannot. If you get crossed up on one of these, it is extremely difficult to get off and the **danger of capsizing here is extreme;** even with two people. With one paddler, and the water is fast moving (as it usually is at high levels) it is next to impossible to get off one of these things safely. Notice again, I said *Very High Water . . .* at normal river flow you would probably never have a problem.

Should you dump, **don't** abandon your canoe unless there is dangerous water *close in front of you.* First grab your paddle, then grab onto the canoe and slowly ease it to shore. Take your time, work *with* the current. **Stay with the canoe** whenever possible.

Regarding the **Big Shoals** area: If you were Portaging (as you should be) you won't have the following problem. However, so you know what to do in case: If you should dump upstream of the shoals and see that you are going to go over, if possible, quickly position yourself at the **stern** of the canoe and in this case hang on (since it is a very short run). Here and any other fast water . . . *always* at the stern; **NEVER** at the bow! You could be smashed between the canoe and a rock if you are hanging onto the bow.

A mistake often made by new canoers (though they learn quickly after they dunk) is pushing off strenuously from a dock or a tree trunk with their paddle. If the paddle slips, over they go. If you must push off with your paddle, do so gently and steadily; all the while maintaining your balance.

If you are solo and see you are about to experience high wind, **don't** paddle from the rear. **(Unless** you have *plenty* of ballast weight to put up front.) If your bow is up in the air it becomes a great sail. It will be next to impossible to maintain your course. Best to paddle from the center on your knees. Kneel, put your butt against the thwart *(not on it)* and spread your knees out as much as possible and still remain comfortable. This will help give you more strength and stability in rough water. *Next best,* paddle from the front. A little more work, but FAR better than stern in wind.

One of the most important things to remember is . . . when you are canoeing, wear your life jacket. **DO NOT** use it as a cushion. If you spill, it's too late to put it on the chances are, you wouldn't be able to get to it anyway.

On the subject of Life Jackets — The State and County laws require there is one life jacket for *every person* in your canoe. They must also be **Coast Guard Approved.** Not long ago, the Coast Guard amended its laws. Now, floating *cushions* **are no longer approved.** In Florida, if you are caught without proper life jackets, it could get expensive. Use a little common sense. Think about it this way . . . never mind the fine . . . it could save your life (or your friend or child).

If you are traveling a strange river for the first time, ask lots of questions of those familiar with the river *before* you go. The more you know about the river, the fewer chances you will have of having a problem. Remember the cliche – Forewarned is Forearmed. Use the Boy Scout's motto and you will rarely have a serious problem. *Be Prepared!* . . . for any emergency. Just don't go overboard. (No pun intended.)

## MORE SAFETY TIPS

It's better to start your trip early in the morning rather than late in the afternoon. You are fresh and your mind is clear. Should you run into some sort of problem, you have the rest of the day to remedy it. Remember, you could get stuck on the river after dark if you cannot find a good campsite. Though canoeing in the dark is not so much of a problem on the mid to lower Suwannee, it definitely could be dangerous on the upper river. Also, finding a campsite in the dark is extremely difficult. It's always best to put down early if you suspect you could have a problem.

Good idea to take a little more water and food than you think you might need. Should you get caught in inclement weather (it could last for several days) and have to lay over; you are prepared for it. Good idea to get a 6-7-day forecast before leaving. That way — no surprises!

If you have the circumstance (as Harry and Ray did in the story) that a person is in trouble in the water . . . I highly recommend you **do not** attempt to bring them into the canoe. If necessary, you can extend your paddle to them and/or throw them a life jacket. Then bring them to the side of your canoe and let them hold on to the side while you work your canoe to shore. However, if circumstances are such that you are too far from shore, the correct way to "boat them" is for them to move to the center of the canoe. Grasp a cross thwart *as far across to the opposite side as possible,* kicking hard lift themselves far enough to get their waist across the gunwale. Then they should lean into the canoe and fall, not attempting to right themselves until after they are completely inside. If you are fully loaded with gear, *be extremely careful.* Circumstances dictate the action taken but if I were loaded and had the above situation, I would have them lay perfectly still once they were on top of my gear. Remember, _now you have become top heavy_ and could easily capsize. While all this is happening, you and your partner (?) should *remain seated* and attempt to counterbalance the off center weight. **DO NOT stand** and/or attempt to grab the person in the water. If you do, you more than likely will join him for a swim.

*I don't expect anyone to remember all of the items mentioned here, however, if you remember just one that helps you have a safe and more enjoyable trip, I have accomplished my intent.*

I hope you have a great trip!

## IMPORTANT PHONE NUMBERS

THE CANOE OUTPOST, LIVE OAK . . . . . . . . . . . . . . . . 1-800-428-4147

"SPIRIT OF THE SUWANNEE" CAMPGROUND OFFICE . . . 904-364-1683

SUWANNEE RIVER WATER MGMT. DISTRICT . . . . . . . . 1-800-226-1066

    Local . . . . . . . . . . . . . . . . . . . . . . . . . . . . . . . . . . . 904-362-1001

SUWANNEE RIVER STATE PARK . . . . . . . . . . . . . . . . 904-362-2746

LIVE OAK CHAMBER OF COMMERCE . . . . . . . . . . . . . 904-362-3071

GRIFFIS FISH CAMP . . . . . . . . . . . . . . . . . . . . . . . . . 912-637-5395
    Upper river put-in <u>above</u> FARGO and below "The Sill."
    Good launch and camping (Run by Arden, Lem's son)

WAL-MART SUPER STORE, LAKE CITY . . . . . . . . . . . . . 904-755-2427

SUWANNEE GABLES MOTEL & MARINA . . . . . . . . . . . . 352-542-7752
    (on the river - in OLDTOWN)

OLDTOWN KOA KAMPGROUND . . . . . . . . . . . . . . . . . . 352-542-7636

YELLOW JACKET CAMPGROUND . . . . . . . . . . . . . . . . . 352-542-8365

TREASURE CAMP GRO. - at FOWLER'S BLUFF . . . . . . . . 352-493-2950

MILLER'S MARINE CAMPGROUND, SUWANNEE . . . . . . . 352-542-7349

OKEFENOKEE NAT'L. WILDLIFE REFUGE **(permits)** . . . . 1-912-496-3331
    **For those wanting to canoe the OKEFENOKEE Swamp**

STEPHEN FOSTER CAMPGROUND - **Reservations** . . . . . . 1-800-864-7275

STEPHEN FOSTER REC. PARK CAMPGROUND - **Office** . . 1-912-637-5274

FARGO SHERIFF'S DEPT. . . . . . . . . . . . . . . . . . . . . . 912-487-5315

CITGO Gas Station, FARGO . . . . . . . . . . . . . . . . . . . . 912-637-5336
    (Loraine - good river information)

CELL PHONE USERS - Check each county you'll be in . . .
    some are on 911 - <u>some not!</u> My cell phone worked fine
    east of the Withlacoochee. Did not try it farther downstream.

If you are unable to find MUSKOL, call . . . . . . . . . . . . . . 1-800-842-4090

---

## NOTES

# — CANOE RENTALS —
## SOME ARE FULL OUTFITTERS

Suwannee Canoe
& Kayak Outfitters
2105 Westfield Dr.
Valdosta, GA 32602
Ben Anderson
Ph. 912-247-0408

Suwannee Canoe Outpost
2461 95th Drive
Live Oak, FL 32060
David Pharr
Ph. 904-364-4991
1-800-428-4147

American Canoe Adventures
Rt. 1 Box 8335
White Springs, FL 32096
Wendell Hannum
Ph. 904-397-1309

Ed's Canoes
PO Box 2038
High Springs, FL 32655
Ed McKinnon
Ph. 904-454-3757

River Run Campground
Rt. 2 Box 811
Branford, FL 32008
Gene Cavaer
Ph. 904-935-1086

Nature Quest
PO Box 2999
Lake City, FL 32056
Jim & Tere Free
Ph. 904-755-5252

Blue Springs Resort
Rt. 1 Box 1950
Lee, FL 32059
Ph. 904-971-2880

Manatee Springs State Park
Rt. 2 Box 617
Chiefland, FL 32626
Ph. 904-393-0726

Miller's Marina
PO Box 280
Suwannee, FL 32692
Ph. 904-542-7349

Suwannee Outdoor
Adventures Center
PO Box 2487
White Springs, FL 32906
Ph. 904-397-2347

Suwannee Plantation
Campground
Rt. 3 Box 73
Oldtown, FL 32680
Gary Clark
Ph. 352-542-8902

Santa Fe Outpost
PO Box 592
High Springs, FL 32655
Jim Wood
Ph. 904-454-2050

Old Florida Guides
and Outfitters
Rt. 1 Box 1895
White Springs, FL 32096
Ph. 904-397-2945

Gennie Springs
7300 NE Gennie Springs Rd.
High Springs, FL 32643
Rhonda Johnson
Ph. 904-454-2202

Steamboat Canoe Outfitters
1220 NE 127th Lane
Branford, FL 32008
Bill Smith
Ph. 904-935-0512

Jim Hollis' River Rendezvous
Rt. 2 Box 60
Mayo, FL 32066
Ph. 904-294-2510

Otter Springs Resort
Rt. 1 Box 1400
Trenton, FL 32693
Ph. 904-263-2696

Call these numbers for rental or outfitting
information or check out their page at
http://www.canoeoutpost.com

## Related Good Reading

**Canoe Camping - An Introductory Guide**
*by Cecil Kuhne* – Paper

**Canoeing and Camping - "Back to Basics"**
*by Cliff Jacobson* – Paper

**Canoe Camping - "Beyond Basics"**
*by Cliff Jacobson* – Paper

**Kayak Camping**
*by David Harrison* – Paper

**Roughing It Elegantly** - A practical guide to Canoe Camping
*by Patricia Bell and Linda Oliver Isakson* – Paper

**Song of the Paddle -**
Illustrated Guide to Wilderness Camping
*by Bill Mason* – Paper

**Guide to Canoe Camping**
*by Bruce D. Johnson* – Paper

**The Canoe Camper's Handbook**
*by Ray Bearse* – Paper

**The Complete Book of Canoe Camping**
*by J. Wayne Fears* – Paper

**The History of the Okefenokee Swamp**
*by A. S. McQueen & Hamp Mizell*

**The Okefenokee Swamp**
*by Franklin Russell*

**The Okefenokee Swamp**
*by Dr. Roland M. Harper*

**Birds of the Okefenokee Swamp**
*by Albert H. Wright & Francis Harper*

**Birds of the Suwannee River**
*by Arthur T. Wayne*

**Fishes of the Okefenokee Swamp**
*by Joshua Laerm & B. J. Freeman*

**Okefenokee: Profiles of the Past**
Okefenokee Wildlife League
Special Publication No. 1, 1998
*by C. T. Trowell*
(It will be available at the bookstore at SCRA soon.)

**Suwannee River - Strange Green Land**
*by Cecile Matschat* – Hard
(Published in **1938** by the Literary Guild of America, it is long out of print - but can still be found *[I recently found two copies on the Internet for friends.]* I couldn't put it down since it described the river, flora and fauna, daily life and customs of the people living inside the Okefenokee swamp in the 1920's.)